THE MODERN NATIONS IN

HISTORICAL PERSPECTIVE

ROBIN W. WINKS, *General Editor*

The volumes in this series deal with individual nations or groups of closely related nations throughout the world, summarizing the chief historical trends and influences that have contributed to each nation's present-day character, problems, and behavior. Recent data are incorporated with established historical background to achieve a fresh synthesis and original interpretation.

MASSIMO SALVADORI, *the author of this volume, was born in London of Italian and British parents and brought up in Italy. Educated in Switzerland, he received his Doctorate in Political Science from the University of Rome. He has taught at the University of Geneva in Switzerland, at St. Lawrence University in Canton, New York, and at Bennington College. Since 1947 Dr. Salvadori has been a member of the faculty of Smith College, where he is now Dwight Morrow Professor of History. Among his works in Italian are books on the problem of liberty and on the Italian Resistance; among those in English are Liberal Democracy, The Economics of Freedom, and Cavour and the Unification of Italy.*

OTHER VOLUMES IN THE EUROPEAN SUBSERIES:

Austria and Hungary *by R. John Rath*
The Balkans *by Charles Jelavich and Barbara Jelavich,* S-611
East Central Europe *by Frederick G. Heymann*
France *by John C. Cairns,* S-617
Germany
Ireland *by Oliver MacDonagh*
Russia *by Robert V. Daniels,* S-602
Scandinavia *by John H. Wuorinen,* S-614
Spain *by Richard Herr*

ITALY AT THE END OF THE FIRST CENTURY B.C.

I T A L Y

Massimo Salvadori

A SPECTRUM BOOK

Prentice-Hall, Inc.

Englewood Cliffs, New Jersey

To those who see nations as the components of the community of man.

PREFACE

This book aims to increase the reader's knowledge of twentieth-century Italy and to clarify the relationship between her past and her present. Knowledge of the country's past is especially relevant to an understanding of present-day Italy because Italy as a nation has existed for a long time, even when there was no Italian state; and, more important, because Italians are keenly aware of their continuity.

Chapter One briefly describes pertinent aspects of the Italian scene in the mid-1960's: Italy's position in connection with world problems; her physical and demographic setting; her economic, intellectual, and political environment; and her relations with other countries. Chapter Eight deals with the crises of 1914-1922, which first weakened and then destroyed the free institutions of the Italian state created in 1859-61. Fascism, the structure of the Fascist state, and Fascist achievements and failures down to 1943 are the topics of Chapter Nine. Chapter Ten describes the upheavals of 1943-46 affecting all aspects of national life and the ensuing experiment in republican democracy until 1964.

The chapters on historical background emphasize the inheritance from the past. Chapter Two describes the cultural unity of the peoples inhabiting Italy, attained through the expansion of the ancient Roman republic and the centuries-long identification of Italy with Rome; the continuing influence of some Latin writers; and legal and political concepts and institutions developed in the Roman state that did not disappear in post-Roman Italy. The territorial fractioning of the Middle Ages, which is at the base of deep-seated regional differences in today's Italy, is described in Chapter Three. Chapter Four deals with Catholicism. Originally the Italian version of Christianity and always per-

v

vading many aspects of Italian life, Catholicism was molded ideologically and institutionally during the early Middle Ages and has been modified but not basically changed since then. In the late Middle Ages today's Italian language took form (Chapter Five); this period also produced the classics on which much of Italian education is founded. In early modern times (Chapter Six) became dominant those traits of the national character acquired under the combined pressure of severe political and spiritual crises. In the nineteenth century (Chapter Seven) most of the Italian nation was united in a single state; then also were born the movements, identified with political forces but transcending politics and standing for distinct ways of life, important in Italy during the most recent decades: nationalism, Christian democracy, and socialism (both democratic and authoritarian), among others. In these chapters mention is also made of what, though important once, has left little or no trace in present-day Italy, from the ancient Romans' code of values to Medieval democratic communes and the individualism of the Renaissance.

The volumes on France, Germany, and Spain in this series will be found useful for placing Italy in her European setting. Because of American and Soviet influence today, direct and indirect, the volumes on the United States and the Soviet Union can also be profitably consulted in relation to Italy.

A few passages have been adapted from some of the author's other writings: "Italy," an article in the Foreign Policy Association *Headline Series*, 87 (May–June 1951); "The End of the Renaissance in Italy," paper published in *The Renaissance Reconsidered* (Northampton, Mass.: Smith College Studies in History, 1964); and *Cavour and the Unification of Italy* (Princeton, N.J.: Van Nostrand, 1961).

The Glossary defines expressions referring specifically to the Italian scene (e.g., clericalism, communes, *Risorgimento*).

M. S.

Contents

ONE

ITALY TODAY

Italy covers an area less than one-thirtieth that of the United States, yet her population is more than one-fourth the size of America's. In 1964 her national income was about a twelfth of the American in dollars of equivalent purchasing power. Jutting into the Mediterranean Sea, Italy is equally close to democratic North Atlantic Europe, to revolutionary Islamic North Africa, and to the Communist states in the Balkans. Economically, her northern regions are on a par with the advanced industrial nations, while her southern regions are on the level of the underdeveloped countries. Despite many elements making for acute tension, for the twenty years since the end of World War II Italy has enjoyed remarkable internal stability within a democratic frame and under prevalently Catholic leadership. Since the formation of the North Atlantic Alliance in 1949, she has been praised by press and radio when clouds have darkened the international scene. At the same time, Italy's reliability as an ally has been doubted by many who are aware of a strong neutralist current and the influence of a powerful Communist party.

Known to Americans as the original homeland of millions of fellow citizens, Italy has since World War II become the goal of great numbers of tourists, familiar through the influence of books and films that have been successful in the United States. Nevertheless, when the average educated American thinks of Italy he thinks mostly of her past. In the case of Italy especially, one needs to distinguish between the community of people, or nation, and the political structure, or state. The Italian nation dates from the time, two thousand and more years ago, when there was a clear-cut separation between the Roman state in Italy and the Roman state outside Italy. Deep crises affected the nation in the fifth, eleventh, and sixteenth centuries, but they did not destroy its continuity. In contrast, though little more than a hundred years old, the Italian state of today has already gone through three distinct phases: monarchical, Fascist, republican.

Italy and the World

Although Italy took a secondary place in European affairs for over four hundred years, she has, for better or worse, played a considerable role in contemporary events in recent decades. Though not a strong industrial or military power, the Italian state has had governments for about a third of its recent existence that have followed nationalistic policies aimed at imperialistic goals. As a result, Italy has directly or indirectly been a major factor in the conflicts of the last half century. Her victory over the Ottoman empire in 1911-12 was an important event in the landslide that led to World War I in 1914. The Italian invasion of Ethiopia in 1935 started another landslide which in 1939 became World War II. During the most tense period of the cold war between the United States and the Soviet Union, Italy played her role. She was a front-line bastion of the system of alliances organized by the United States between 1947 and 1955 to resist the pressure of a Communist bloc not yet weakened by the Soviet-Chinese rift.

Americans have known fascism mainly as a German phenomenon, but it was born in Italy among a group of irresponsible extremists fired with nationalist frenzy and moved by unbridled hatred for the Liberal democratic state. Its success in Italy inspired imitators in scores of other countries. The ambitions of fascism and the great emotional upheaval it created caused, in World War II, some of the worst massacres ever known. Under varying names, fascism is still alive in all movements in which nationalism is obsessive, and which aim at a totalitarian organization of the national community through the one-party state, the complete subordination of all citizens to their ruler, glorification of the leader, absolute control over minds, economic autarchy, and the elimination of uncomfortable minorities—ethnic, social, religious, or other.

Italy is the center of Roman Catholicism, which is not only a creed but an all-embracing way of life. With its half-billion adherents and its half-million clergy, it is one of the most influential forces in the world today. Italians played a primary role in molding the ideology and institutions of Catholicism through the centuries, and also in its contemporary revival, discussed below. Catholics form a majority, sometimes the whole population, in over a fourth of the world's independent states. In another ten, including the United States and some of the English-speaking members of the Commonwealth, they constitute influential, perhaps soon dominant, minorities.

Italy is today the home of one of the biggest and most important Communist parties outside Communist-controlled countries. The party is supported by large sections of the middle class and peasantry, and by smaller sections of the industrial wage-earners. Communism appeals to many Italian intellectuals, who see in it the only road to progress, prosperity, and happiness. On the municipal level the Italian Communist party is often powerful, and the possibility of a Communist take-over is mentioned whenever a crisis grips the country. Italian Communist leaders enjoy considerable prestige in the international Communist movement; at times they have exercised a restraining influence over their Soviet colleagues, and they have been active in mediating between Soviet and Chinese Communists. Communism has been a factor in the steady growth of neutralism in Italy.

For the last three generations Italians have emigrated in large numbers, and their descendants abroad form communities which (at least culturally) often keep in touch with the country of origin. There are now millions of Americans of Italian descent; they are becoming more and more prominent in the political, intellectual, and economic life of the United States. Possibly as much as a third of the population of Argentina is of Italian origin, and nearly a fifth of the population of Brazil. In Canada, Chile, Mexico, Uruguay, and Venezuela Italians form important segments of the population. There was a period in 1964 when the presidents of five Latin American republics had names revealing their Italian origin. There are large Italian communities in Belgium, France, Switzerland, and West Germany; also in some African countries.

Land and People

Italy is about the size of Arizona. Except for a short stretch in the northeast, natural boundaries are clearly marked by seas and mountains. About two-fifths of the total area forms continental, or northern, Italy, an irregular rectangle less than three hundred miles long and two hundred miles wide with France to the west and Yugoslavia to the east. Continental Italy is for the most part a vast, fertile, well-irrigated plain sloping eastward to the Adriatic Sea, and encircled to the west and north, and partly to the east, by the towering and wooded Alps and to the south by the lower and barren Apennines. Nature gives unity to continental Italy and favors the development of homogeneous communities.

South of continental Italy lies the slightly larger peninsula, over five hundred miles long, dividing the Mediterranean into a western and an eastern basin. The backbone of the peninsula is formed by the Apennine range. Except for a few small coastal and inland plains, the peninsula is hilly. Rivers are numerous but have little water, and there are few lakes. As in Greece (but less so), mountains and hills divide the peninsula into separate and varied districts where, in the past, communities tended to evolve independently.

The island of Sicily (slightly smaller than Vermont) is a natural stepping-stone between Italy and Tunisia, less than one hundred miles away. Sardinia (about the size of New Hampshire) was until quite recent times somewhat isolated, and it developed its own particular culture. Both islands are mountainous and poor in water. Historians influenced by geographical determinism see in Italy's central position in the Mediterranean, varied terrain, and temperate climate factors explaining her historical growth, her cultural diversity, and the political fragmentation lasting from the sixth to the nineteenth century.

Italy's population at the beginning of 1965 was just over fifty-two million (about 28 per cent of the U.S. population in the same year). Numerically, Italy is the third largest Western European nation. The birth rate (below 2 per cent in the early Sixties) and the natural increase of the population (less than 1 per cent) are moderate. Italy's population—in a slightly larger area—is nearly two and a half times what it was when most of the country was united politically in 1859-60. In parts of continental Italy, and in some plains of peninsular

Italy and Sicily, the population density reaches 2,000 per square mile. It is low in mountain areas, in some formerly malarial coastal districts, and in most of Sardinia. Since the end of World War II there has been a sizable movement away from mountains and hills toward the plains, away from rural areas toward the cities, away from the under-developed south toward the industrial northwestern regions. Less than a fourth of the population now lives in the countryside; about a fifth lives in the ten largest cities, of which four have more than a million inhabitants (Rome has about two and one-half million). The rest live in hundreds of medium-sized and small cities and thousands of villages.

Italians are a nation but not a homogeneous race. Culture and tradition, not biological traits, give them unity. In the southern third of the country the Mediterranean type predominates; in the other two-thirds the Alpine type is common, except in the northeast where Dynaric and Nordic influences have diluted the Alpine characteristics.

Since 1945, when the northeastern areas annexed after World War I went to Yugoslavia, ethnic minorities again, as they did before 1918, number less than one per cent of the total population. Half of these are German-speaking communities in northeastern Italy, a quarter are French-speaking communities in the northwest, and the remaining quarter are mainly Albanians and Greeks scattered through the southern regions. In Italy only a few racists consider the small Jewish community, several tens of thousands, as ethnically different from other Italians.

Although forming a single national unit, Italians are highly differentiated according to geographical-historical regions. Regional dialects (some having their own distinctive literature) show great diversity. Italians of all classes are aware of a contrast between northern Italy, culturally close to the nations of northwestern Europe, and southern Italy where the way of life is typically Mediterranean, with central Italy holding an intermediate position.

Northern Italy, inhabited by about half of the population, consists of eight geographical-historical regions. Here, in the Middle Ages, developed the powerful and wealthy merchant republics of Venice and Genoa in Venetia and Liguria respectively, and the duchy of Milan, which included most of Lombardy. Here, in modern times, evolved the Piedmontese state, which played a primary role in the unification of Italy in the nineteenth century. Central Italy, the northern part of the peninsula, contains five regions. One is Latium, once a small district around and south of Rome, then Rome's partner in the conquests leading to the formation of the Roman empire in the ancient Mediterranean world. Another central Italian region is Tuscany, whose chief city, Florence, once a republic, played in Italy from the thirteenth to the sixteenth century the role that Athens had played nearly two thousand years earlier in the intellectual and political life of ancient Greece. The rest of the peninsula (five regions), and the two major islands forming southern Italy, were in ancient times (except Sardinia) the home of a vigorous branch of Greek civilization, and in early modern times a stagnant dependency of the far-flung Spanish empire.

Inaccurate as generalizations about national character must inevitably be, few would deny that the human environment in Italy is different from that of other European nations, and that differences go deeper than language and customs. Though there are of course all sorts of Italians, a prevailing "Italian type" does exist. It was molded in the stagnant authoritarian society that emerged from the intellectual and political crises of the sixteenth century (see Chapter Six). It is the type foreigners have in mind when they speak of "the Italians," identifying the part with the whole. It is easily described: extroverted, rather emotional but seldom hysterical, skeptical, contemptuous of authority in words but in fact subservient, considerate of others often to the point of seeming hypocritical, gregarious, somewhat devious, quick-minded, enduring. The combination of considerateness, skepticism, and deviousness makes for courtesy and often, at the same time, unreliability. Selfishness and arrogance are common traits among those in a position of authority. Servility among those in a position of inferiority is largely compensated for by practical (as distinct from intellectual) humanism: a genuine respect for the individual and genuine willingness to help those in need. Eliminated from the political structure, traditional authoritarianism is still present in many traits of the national character.

There is much family solidarity in all classes, involving collateral as well as lineal relatives. American sociologists have seen in "familism" a main feature of the distinctive Italian way of life. In the more sophisticated sectors of the middle and upper classes, foreigners are often disliked and foreign ways despised, but for most Italians the foreigner is a friend. Patriotism, like national loyalty, is largely a matter of educational level: deeply felt among educated people (whose nationalism often transcends other political values), it declines as one passes to the less educated and the illiterate. On the other hand the weaker the patriotism, the stronger are the indifference to national origins and the sense of human brotherhood.

Mobility—whether simply migration from village to city or the more complex and meaningful movement up and down the social ladder—is transforming the Italian nation. Class differences are nevertheless still sharp, and subdivisions numerous. Tradition rather than economic activity accounts for the social classes, often rooted in a far past which may go back to ancient times. In many communities of central and southern Italy, where the full impact of modern civilization has yet to be felt, the class structure and class relationships date back two millennia or more and remain nearly as deeply embedded as they were then. A too-rigid class structure has been an obstacle to the development of the nation in modern times, and its adjustment to a contemporary world that demands flexibility.

Out of nearly thirteen million families, fewer than a million belong to the influential groups of the population forming what in Europe is called the ruling class. Of these groups the largest is the intelligentsia —the professional and intellectual sections of the middle class. By virtue of training and occupation, the large and influential Catholic clergy belongs to this group. Two smaller groups are an upper middle class of successful business people, and a nobility composed mainly of big and medium-sized landowners—descendants of those who once formed the ruling oligarchies of independent regional states, the builders of palaces and villas admired by the tourists.

As elsewhere in Europe, the intelligentsia has for generations been the most dynamic element of the population. From professional people and intellectuals came those who in the eighteenth century welcomed the ideas of the Enlightenment and of the French Revolution; most of the nineteenth century liberals and patriots who engaged in the struggle for national unity and free institutions known as the *Risorgimento*; and those who sometimes ably, sometimes less so, ran the affairs of the nation in the post-unification period of liberal ascendancy (1861-1922). Today the intelligentsia provides the leadership for all the movements important in the country, from political Catholicism to communism, from neo-fascism to socialism. Since the end of World War II, every single important figure in Italian political life has been a member of the intelligentsia—professor, journalist, cleric, lawyer, writer, or scientist.

There is a sharp cleavage in Italy between what Europeans call the lower middle class (the petty bourgeoisie of collectivist jargon) and all other social classes, above and below. The lower middle class includes the very small, often minute, business people: the independent storekeepers (too numerous today and consequently poor), the artisans or craftsmen who own their shops and perhaps a small amount of machinery, the contractors and middlemen operating on a shoestring. It also includes the lower ranks of white-collar employees, the minor officials of private enterprises and public administration. The lower middle class is probably larger than either of the two main subdivisions of the lower, or working, class—industrial wage-earners and peasants. It accounts for more than a quarter of the population, about four million families in the early Sixties. Artisans are rapidly declining in numbers and soon may quite disappear; but on the other hand more and more skilled wage-earners are losing their proletarian characteristics and adopting lower middle class mentality and customs. The passing of manual workers from the lower classes to the petty bourgeoisie is as much psychological as economic, and here education plays a dominant role. Industrious and energetic, ambitious and imaginative, the lower middle class is an economic asset to the nation. It has provided the vast majority of entrepreneurs responsible for the industrial boom of the postwar period. Politically, in acquiring a consciousness which had not existed since the end of the Middle Ages, the lower middle class has provided a fertile ground for nationalism, fascism, and racism in the Twenties and Thirties, for communism and neo-fascism in the present generation.

With the partial exception of the more skilled group mentioned above, nonagricultural wage-earners form the urban lower class, nearly as large as the petty bourgeoisie. Educationally handicapped but using their innate intelligence, their main concern is economic security and moderate economic improvement. Indifferent, now as in the past, to the appeal of nationalism, they form the mass of the three main Italian labor organizations, one controlled by Communists and fellow-traveling Socialists, the second by democratic Socialists and non-Socialist Democrats, the third by Catholics.

Excluding the landowner class—which owns land and exploits it through the labor of others—a little more than a quarter of the population (about three and one-half million families) lives off the produce of the land. They form the peasantry, the rural and agricultural lower class. A generation ago peasants still formed half of the Italian population. The postwar industrial boom created openings which they have been happy to fill, and for the last twenty years peasants have been leaving the rural areas in numbers that recall the flight from the farms in England at the end of the eighteenth century. Intellectuals may sing the praises of country life and find farms and pastures charming, but those who have known the hardship of too much work in the fields, the meager return, and the insecurity caused by uncertain weather and uncertain markets, are glad to escape. The postwar industrial boom (like the boom early in the century) was facilitated by the cheap labor of former peasants, for whom a low industrial wage was always more than what they could get from the soil. In spite of this mass exodus of millions during the last two decades, there still are more farms in Italy than in the United States, and too many people still live off the land. In 1964 it was estimated that the Italian peasantry as a whole would not have a satisfactory standard of living until two million more peasants had abandoned agriculture. A large percentage of peasants own the land they cultivate (in most cases only a few acres, quite inadequate for providing a family with a decent standard of living). Others are tenants, share-croppers, and laborers, numerous in northern, central, and southern Italy respectively. In 1963-65 measures were taken by the government to end the uneconomical and politically dangerous share-cropping system.

Economics

In the early 1960's the Italian labor force accounted for only 40 per cent of the population, a lower percentage than that shown by any census for fifty years. Besides the already mentioned 27 per cent of the labor force engaged in agriculture, 41 per cent was engaged in secondary industries and 32 per cent in tertiary or service industries. Since 1951, the percentage had declined by about a third in agriculture, and increased by about a third in the services and a fourth in industry. Salary- and wage-earners accounted for only 52.5 per cent of the labor forces, almost the same as twenty years earlier (51.5 per cent). Italian statistics put in the same category the bulk of the lower middle class who exploit their capital with their own labor, and *mezzadri* (share-croppers), who usually own part of the capital needed for the exploitation of the land. The two categories accounted for 33.1 per cent of the labor force—a decrease of about one-fifth since 1943. The remaining 14.4 per cent included entrepreneurs, salaried executives, and professional people. In Italy, salary- and wage-earners represent a smaller proportion of the labor force than in the three most advanced industrial nations of the West: the United States, Great Britain, and West Germany. For a long period the unemployed had been about a tenth of the labor force: by the early 1960's they had dropped to about a thirtieth. Underemployment had declined a great deal in the southern agricultural communities but was still high.

By 1964 the Italian gross national product (GNP) had reached the figure of about forty billion dollars (in real terms twice that of 1953, which in turn, in spite of heavy destruction caused by the war, was about half as much again as the pre-World War II GNP). Taking into account the different way of life, the different concept of what constitutes necessities, and the fact that prices of some essential articles and of most services were lower than in the United States, the forty billion dollars were the equivalent of nearly a third as much again. This would put the 1964 Italian GNP at about one-twelfth of the American. Not counting the contribution of public expenses, industry supplied almost half of the GNP, services one-third, and agriculture less than one-fifth. Foreign trade played a proportionally greater role in the Italian than in the American economy. Foreign investments, American and European, had stimulated economic growth. Tourism, shipping, and remittances from emigrants had for many years been important elements in the Italian balance of payments, but in 1963 and 1964 they were not enough to cover the deficit caused by imports. The fact that Italians, striving for a higher standard of living, tended to consume more than they produced, had caused a minor recession which led to a temporary restriction in consumption. In 1964 private and public investments accounted for about one-sixth of the Italian GNP, a higher percentage than the average in America.

Figures on production, consumption, and exchange should be seen in the light of the institutional structure and functioning of the Italian economy. Formally, even after the disappearance of Fascist corporatism, the Italian postwar economy was essentially a modernized version of mercantilism: an economy in which most of the means of production and exchange were owned privately, and in which the use of such means was largely controlled and guided by the state through taxes, fees, tariffs, and labor and social legislation. In reality, the private sector, which produced over four-fifths of the total output of goods and services, operated with considerable autonomy, and the internal market, thanks to lax enforcement of regulations, was essentially free. This apparent contradiction between theory and reality was largely the result of governmental inability to enforce controls and provide guidance.

In the private sector, much of the artisan activity operated within the frame of a pre-capitalistic individual-exchange economy. Agricultural activities were in part carried out within the simpler frame of a domestic economy (production mainly for home consumption). Cooperatives were negligible. The remainder formed a vigorous and dynamic capitalistic sector of the economy—a field in which hundreds of thousands of entrepreneurs operated. The relatively low percentage of salary- and wage-earners shows that in Italy ownership of the means of production is widespread; however, the diffusion is very uneven. Less than a fifth of the capital available in the country was divided into minute fractions belonging to several million independent producers and middlemen. All the rest was concentrated in a few tens of thousands of corporations belonging to a comparatively small group of owners. The Italian giant corporations are huger, in relation to Italy's wealth, than American giant corporations.

Some of the biggest Italian corporations are owned by the state, to which belong about half of the steel industry, an eighth of the mechanical industries, and most of the chemical industry, banks, insurance businesses, etc. The public sector of industry (employing nearly 300,000 workers) contributed by the mid-1960's about a tenth of the total Italian industrial output. If to the state-owned industries one adds railroads, shipping, airlines, the communication media (including radio and television, which are state monopolies), educational and health services, enterprises owned by the military forces, public lands, and an imposing mass of buildings, the publicly owned capital (and the public share in output of goods and services) is greater, relative to the economy, in Italy than in any other noncollectivist country. Judging by the remarkable growth and efficiency of private enterprise since the end of World War II, the prosperity of the entrepreneurial class, and the increase in real wages in private employment, Italian capitalism has not suffered from the presence of state socialism. Both have expanded and flourished, to the general advantage of the Italian nation.

In Italy economic conditions vary considerably from region to region. In the northwest, the so-called industrial triangle between Milan, Turin and Genoa is as prosperous as neighboring France and almost as prosperous as neighboring Switzerland. In the south, Sardinia and Basilicata are nearly as poor as the neighboring North African and Balkan countries. The equivalent of $500 a year is a large income for a southern laborer, while a skilled worker in the north normally earns five to six times as much. Economic conditions vary even more by social classes. There is less redistribution of income through taxation and public services in Italy than in the nations of northwestern Europe. Many Catholic institutions (bishoprics, religious orders) and foundations, many industrialists and some titled landowners have huge fortunes and large incomes. According to a government survey, more than ten million Italians are poor (the Italian definition of poverty starts, statistically, at a much lower level than the American one), lacking adequate food and shelter. The mention of poverty should not, however, obscure the progress made in the postwar period. Since the end of World War II, Italians—with the often forgotten contribution of American aid—have probably achieved as much as was humanly possible in the economic field. Considering their resources, they have made bigger strides than either collectivist nations or advanced capitalist nations like the United States and Great Britain. For all that, tension has not abated.

Intellectual Diversity

The disruption of state and society at the end of World War II gave rise to greater liberty and hence to an emancipation of individual energies. This, along with many other factors of course, favored the postwar economic expansion and the transformation of material life. The same liberty favored the postwar intellectual vigor revealed through literary and artistic achievements, through lively discussions, through the progress of education. Intellectual emancipation and dynamism led to a change within the Italian nation in the relative importance of ways of thinking which, at a high level of sophistication, are usually formulated as complex and involved philosophies, and at the general level of mass diffusion are often uncomplicated conceptual frameworks. The latter, anchored to a few basic ideas and values more or less unconsciously taken for granted, regulate everyday activities; the former often contribute to the direction of long-range trends. At both levels the Italian nation lacks uniformity. When it comes to ways of thinking, differences between sections of the population are more in kind than in degree. Involving divergent views of man and society, they make for antagonistic ways of life. The difficulty of finding a satisfactory formula for peaceful coexistence is a source of tension, and no one can clearly predict the final outcome of the changes now taking place.

It is usual to think of Italy as a Catholic nation. More than a religious creed, Catholicism is a way of life founded on a well integrated system of concepts and values, and expressed through a definite set of institutions. As a way of life, Catholicism has not had a monopoly over the Italian nation since the middle of the eighteenth century. At present only a minority of Italians are believers (practicing and nonpracticing) to the extent of following their Church in the religious and non-religious fields. This minority accounts for between a third and two-fifths of the nation. Non-Catholic believers are few: less than a hundred thousand Protestants and Jews. The rest of the Italians are agnostics, atheists, or just indifferent. They easily accept as ways of thinking positions that are non-Catholic and often non-Christian. However, the picture is now changing.

For several generations following the collapse of Spanish domination, up until the end of the nineteenth century, Catholicism had been weakening in Italy both as a creed and as a way of thinking. Under the impact of emphasis on scientific knowledge and the scientific method, and of the ensuing discoveries and inventions, ways of thinking that either ignored or denied the Divinity had gained ground among educated Italians.

Now the trend has been reversed. The reversal took its impulse from the process of clarification of Catholic thought, and restatement of Catholic principles, that has been going on for a hundred years or so (see Chapter Four). The process led first to the elimination of various deviations linked to ways of thinking that had developed among non-Catholics outside Italy, from the nineteenth century Rosminianism imbued with idealism to twentieth century positivistic modernism. The process has led since the beginning of the century to a vigorous Catholic intellectual counteroffensive which has borne fruit in this postwar period.

The position of scholasticism as the exclusive philosophical foundation of Italian Catholicism has been reaffirmed, in its improved neo-Thomistic interpretation, since the encyclical *Aeterni Patris* of 1879. The distinction between a theological field in which revelation rules, and a philosophical field in which reason is used, makes it possible for Italian Catholics to accept the findings of modern science and to contribute to scientific research. An ontological position is consistent with the neo-Thomist postulate that revelation and reason will finally reach identical conclusions, and is implicit in the role reason plays in Catholic thinking. In its theism, realism, and objectivism, as much as in its trust in formal logic, neo-Thomism differs sharply from all other ways of thinking influential in European nations since the middle of the eighteenth century—from scientific empiricism, materialism, and positivism as from idealism, voluntarism, and existentialism. The application of scholastic formal logic to revealed dogmas tends to render neo-Thomistic thought static and rigid: changes, like those taking place at present, are seldom due to an inner process; they are usually an adaptation to strong pressures coming from non-Catholic sources. The static rigidity of the Catholic way of thinking makes for the conservatism which is the main feature of Italian political Catholicism. The Catholic effort to achieve the kind of society in which change is reduced to a minimum appeals, independently of religious considerations, to millions of Italians who prefer the quiet and peace of a static society to the tensions of a dynamic one.

Non-Italians have had their share in the contemporary revision and clarification of Catholic thought, but the main contribution comes from Italian Catholics: from the Vatican Curia through a number of carefully prepared encyclicals, through official statements on contemporary problems, and through the proclamation of new dogmas; from members of monastic orders, Augustinians, Dominicans, Franciscans, Jesuits; from many distinguished laymen; from teachers in rapidly expanding Catholic universities. The Sacred Heart University, founded in the early 1920's in Milan—one of the few private institutions of higher learning in Italy—has prepared many of the postwar Italian leaders. Important for practical purposes has been the formulation of a Catholic approach in the social disciplines. To classical, neoclassical, and collectivist economics one must now add Catholic economics. A. Fanfani, several times prime minister, is an influential thinker in this field. There is a Catholic political science just as there is Catholic sociology, Catholic anthropology, Catholic psychology, and so on.

Before the advent of fascism in the early Twenties, papal pilgrimages to Italian and foreign shrines, public religious processions, participation of the Catholic clergy in all or most official manifestations, Catholic religious teaching in public schools, state-enforced Catholic supervision over publications and other communications media, were unthinkable. Now they are routine. In the relations between Church and state, between clergy and nation, there is a revolution in process that is radically altering the institutional structure of Italy. Its impact is being felt in education, in economic and social legislation, in all communications media. It is also felt in the conduct of foreign affairs.

In the field of conceptual frameworks, dialectical materialism—Marxism in various interpretations—is the strongest opponent in Italy of Catholic neo-Thomistic ontologism. Dialectical materialism denies neo-Thomism *in toto* through basic principles such as the monistic view of the universe and life, the reality of matter only, the substitution for the Divinity of laws immanent in matter itself as an explanation for what the mind does not grasp, the making of a mental process (the dialectical method) the fundamental law of life, the vision of a determined universe. Each basic principle is as much of a dogma as revealed truths are for Italian Catholics. Dialectical materialism also denies neo-Thomism *in toto* through its rejection of formal logic, replaced by the simpler rules of dialectical thinking. By postulating the end of change once communism has been established, dialectical materialism restricts to the point of nullification its own theoretical dynamism. The postulates and method forming the frame of dialectical materialism differ completely from those of neo-Thomism, but the two ways of thinking have certain features in common. Both are fundamentally static and rigid. As a result, dialogues between dialectical materialists and neo-Thomists are merely dull exchanges of monologues; neither side can make an impression on the other, and a mental wall separates the two major sections of the Italian nation.

Dialectical materialism was fostered by the small section of the intelligentsia that embraced socialism in the last two decades of the nineteenth century. It fitted into the groove prepared by positivism, at that time dominant among educated non-Catholic Italians. It was influenced by the pre-World War I debate between revisionists and orthodox Marxists, and later by the debate between Leninists and anti-Leninists. Of course there are no reliable data to judge by, but it is possible that a plurality, if not a majority, of the Italian intelligentsia—including some of the best-known names in every field of intellectual endeavor—are Marxists. In its revised Leninist interpretation, dialectical materialism forms a coherent and well-integrated system of concepts and values, satisfactory for the many who accept its postulates and methods, fascinating for the ever-growing number of the young who try to find their way in a world in turmoil. Some of the best magazines in Italy are published, and some of the best writing is done, by intellectuals whose minds operate within the frame of reference of dialectical materialism. As in the economic field both capitalism and state socialism have expanded in postwar Italy, so in the field of intellectual activities have both Catholic neo-Thomism and Marxist materialism expanded and increased in influence.

Before the revival of Catholicism and the diffusion of dialectical materialism, positivism and idealism held sway as influences on the thinking of the fast-expanding educated classes. French-inspired deterministic positivism prevailed over the British-inspired empirical

variety. Under conditions of freedom of expression like those existing before 1922, criticism had already corroded positivism. The latter
waned to the point of extinction during the 1930's, when fascism
suppressed periodicals taking a positivistic point of view, and when
teachers who were proponents of positivism were barred from schools
and universities.

Idealism became influential later than positivism in Italian life. In
a version stressing the irrational components of the human personality, such as instincts and emotions, it provided the conceptual framework within which nationalists and Fascists formulated their ideas
and aspirations. In a neo-Hegelian version (best known through the
works of the philosopher and historian Croce), stressing both the
spirit and relativism, it was for more than a generation one of the
strongest influences in Italian intellectual life. It survived under fascism and waned in the postwar period, giving ground before Catholicism and materialism.

Empiricism and pragmatism—dominant in most English-speaking
nations in recent generations—never made much headway in Italy,
where there is little inclination toward positions that, while accepting
its limitations, recognize the priority of reason over nonreason; stress
analysis instead of synthesis, and induction instead of deduction;
doubt absolutes; and prefer the scientific method to the Catholics'
formal logic or Marxist dialectics. Galileo is greatly admired by Italians, but he never had the influence in Italy that such thinkers as
Locke and Newton, Dewey and Russell had in English-speaking communities. Skepticism, more than criticism, at times weakens the absolutes which are the pillars of Italian thought.

The Political Scene

The relationship between thought and action (leaving aside the
academic question of which comes first) is a key to understanding
the Italian political scene. Policies, and the political movements behind them, are influenced not only by interests but also by values
and viewpoints inherent in each system of thought. Positivism in its
various interpretations and neo-Hegelian idealism were the respective
ways of thinking of left- and right-wing pre-Fascist liberals, irrational
idealism that of the Fascists. Today, Christian Democracy corresponds
at the practical or political level to Catholic ontologism, its postulates

and its method. To the various schools of materialism correspond as many Socialist parties.

Italian Democrats were not sufficiently numerous or strong in 1945-47 to establish by themselves a democratic republic, such as was voted by a majority of the constituent assembly elected in 1946. The Democrats were helped by two main factors; a balance which compelled antagonistic forces to accept the compromises implicit in democratic procedure, and the presence of Allied troops. At the referendum of June 2, 1946, a slight majority composed of Communists, Socialists, Democrats, and some Catholics, voted in favor of a republican form of government (about twelve million votes to more than ten million in favor of a monarchy). A constituent assembly was elected the same day.

Italy's republican constitution was approved by the constituent assembly on December 22, 1947, with 453 votes to 62, and came into force the following January first. It is a long document containing 157 articles. The first twelve, in which general principles are expressed, are mainly a juxtaposition of the views of the three main tendencies represented in the constituent assembly (Catholicism, socialism closely allied then to communism, and democracy). The statements that sovereignty belongs to the people, that all citizens are equal, that the state guarantees civil liberties, are of democratic inspiration. To socialism and communism are due the statements that labor is the foundation of the republic, that economic obstacles to equality must be eliminated, and that all citizens must contribute to social effort. The declaration concerning the sovereignty of the Catholic Church, and the stress on the difference between Catholic and non-Catholic creeds, are of Catholic derivation, as is the inclusion in the constitution of the Concordat between the Fascist government and the papacy signed in 1929.

Forty-two articles of the constitution deal in detail with the rights and duties of the citizens. They lack the clarity and positiveness of the American Ten Amendments. The fifty-nine articles dealing with the organization of the state establish a parliamentarian form of government. The three branches of government are separate, but the executive is subordinated to the legislative. The functions of head of state (president of the republic) and head of government (prime minister) are separate. The head of state nominates the prime minister who, with his cabinet, assumes his functions only after having received a vote of confidence from the majority of the bicameral parliament. Elections take place on the basis of proportional representation. Half a million voters have the right to ask a national referendum on any subject except the budget, amnesties, and the ratification of international treaties. In exceptional cases parliament can delegate legislative powers to the executive.

Twenty articles concern the organization of the score of geographical-historical regions into which the country is divided, the ninety-one administrative provinces, and nearly eight thousand communes or municipalities.

Regional self-government was first granted to the two large islands of Sicily (nearly five million inhabitants) and Sardinia (one and one-half million). Later it was granted to the French-speaking Val d'Aosta in the northwest; to the Trentino-Alto Adige in the north, where a German-speaking (Austrian) minority accounts for nearly a third of the population; and to Friuli-Julian Venetia in the northeast. The granting of self-government to the other fifteen regions was one of the three main points in the program of the Catholic-Socialist coalition government formed at the end of 1963 and reorganized in 1964. Catholics had been enthusiastic supporters of regional autonomy in 1947. Their enthusiasm waned in the measure in which Communist strength increased. Already in Sicily the regional government had been briefly controlled by an anti-Catholic coalition which included all parties from the extreme right to the extreme left. On the basis of the 1964 returns in the municipal elections, it had become evident that in at least four of the fifteen regions which had not yet achieved regional autonomy power would be in the hands of a communist-led coalition. The four regions accounted for nearly a fifth of Italy's population. Aemilia, the largest, is also one of the most advanced areas of Italy, economically and educationally.

The resurgence of political Catholicism has been the most significant feature of postwar Italy. Survivors of the Catholic Popular party (founded in 1919, collaborator of fascism in 1922, outlawed by the Fascist dictatorship in 1926) organized the Christian Democratic party in 1943. Since December 1945, when the Catholic leader De Gasperi became prime minister, Christian Democracy has been the dominant element in Italian politics. Its electoral strength has varied from 35.2 per cent of the total vote to 48.5 per cent. As an average it can count on the support of almost all believing Catholics (less than two-fifths of the nation), and of conservative groups that are indifferent to Catholicism but see in Christian Democracy the strongest bulwark against subversive leftist forces.

Christian Democracy is essentially a confessional party cutting across social and regional lines. Class interests, divergent views on important internal and external problems, local politics, personal loyalties—all influence the many trends (currents, in Italian political terminology) existing within the party. Obedience to the papacy, as source of authority and as interpreter of the Catholic position, gives the party cohesion. Divisive tendencies failed to split it during the first two decades of its existence, and they probably will not do so in the future. The Italian parties that hope for a break-up of Christian Democracy are likely to be disappointed.

A continual regrouping goes on in the Christian Democratic party, but three major currents can be distinguished. The large and influential clerical right wing is made up of Catholics who would like to see re-established in Italian life the earlier monopoly of the Church. Clericals achieved control of the Christian Democratic party in 1960 and were able to form a coalition cabinet with non-Catholic rightist groups. The cabinet fell as the result of street demonstrations, accompanied by some bloodshed, which were organized by Democrats, Socialists, and Communists. The somewhat smaller left wing is close, on economic and social problems, to the Socialists and, in some sectors, to the Communists. In international affairs, it advocates neutralism. It is tinged with filo-Sovietism.

Between the two wings is the large moderate center, which accepts democratic procedures and, within the frame of democratic institutions, works for recognition of the predominant position of the Catholic Church, religious instruction in the schools, the defense of the family (particularly through uncompromising opposition to divorce), a sound monetary policy, New Dealish or even welfare-state social legislation, limited agrarian reform, protection of the state against communism, collaboration with the United States, and strengthening of Western European solidarity.

It was reckoned in 1963 that out of about thirteen million Christian Democratic voters, some three million were on the side of the left wing, with the rest divided between the center majority and the clerical minority. Labor, cultural, youth, and womens' organizations add to the strength of the Christian Democratic party, which participates actively in a Catholic political international, the International Union of Christian Democrats (first established in 1947) that includes a number of European and Latin American parties.

Whatever the year-by-year platform, Italian Catholics, irrespective of class differences, evaluate and approve of Christian Democracy in relation to ultimate goals which do not need to be expressed in political programs because they are implicit in political Catholicism. These goals include: the strengthening of the Catholic Church vis-à-vis the state, and the gradual elimination of non-Catholic influences in Italy's religious and intellectual life; an economy from which capitalistic competitiveness and collectivist coercion are removed; a policy of peace limited by the necessity of checking the aggressiveness of anti-Catholic forces; and the consolidation of Italy's position as the center of the Catholic world. Only a minority of Italian Catholics looked with favor at the attempts made during the first session of the Ecumenical Council Vatican II, by prelates mostly from countries where Catholics were a minority, to alter the traditional position and structure of their Church.

What holds Italian political Catholicism together (religious discipline) has proved in the postwar period stronger than what divides it (economic interests and foreign policy). The opposite is true of Italian socialism—using this term in its general and all-embracing pre-World War I sense. What Italian Socialists have in common (egalitarianism, communalism, collectivism, materialism, and hatreds focused on myths called "bourgeoisie" and "capitalism") is weaker than what divides them: the problem of liberty and the position adopted in relation to free democratic institutions. The division has been implicit in the dual view of Western European socialism since its earliest days: some Socialists saw socialism as the fulfillment of the liberal revolutions of the eighteenth and nineteenth centuries; for others it was their negation.

Even before 1914, Marxist Socialists (the largest Socialist group in Italy, and founders in 1892 of the Italian Socialist party) were divided. There were those who, accepting democracy as political liberty, also accepted a pluralistic society of which socialism would be

just one element. Others—then the bulk of the Socialist movement
—denied political liberty to non-Socialists; rejected social, political,
and intellectual pluralism, but wanted democratic institutions for a
monistic Socialist society; and meanwhile insisted on democratic procedure within the Socialist movement. And there was a third group,
as monistic as the second, but which rejected democratic procedure
among Socialists in favor of centralized total control from above. At
the level of practical politics this division meant that the first group
was willing to enter the political game in a parliamentarian state and
to collaborate with non-Socialist parties; it could do this only by renouncing integral collectivism and advocating economic and social
reforms acceptable to non-Socialists. (From this group came the
minimalisti or Social Democrats, expelled from the Socialist party
in 1912.) The second group refused to play the parliamentarian game,
was opposed to any kind of collaboration with non-Socialists, but
counted on universal suffrage to put socialism in power (wrongly
postulating that all wage-earners are Socialists and that in Italy industrial wage-earners were a majority). The third group counted on
force to seize power and to replace capitalism with collectivism. This
description is somewhat simplified, but it may help to explain what
Italian socialism is today, and what have been the central themes
in the divisions among Italian Socialists.

Before the secession which led to the formation of the Communist
party in 1921, and the democratic Socialists' decision to go it alone
in 1922, the three groups were known in Italy as *riformisti, massimalisti,* and *rivoluzionari* respectively. From 1947 to the early 1960's
they corresponded to the Social Democratic, Socialist, and Communist parties. Although they were sincere supporters of democratic liberty for Socialists, post-World War I *massimalisti* and the post-World
War II Socialist party denied it to non-Socialists, and therefore, until
the 1956 crisis, stood basically for an authoritarian version of socialism.
Continual groupings and regroupings of Socialist tendencies, secessions, expulsions, and amalgamations have been features of Italian
socialism.

When World War II ended, the Communists, ably led by Togliatti from the late 1920's until his death in 1964, had a strong organization. Authoritarian and democratic Socialists coexisted uneasily
in one party—reorganized in 1943—which was led by Nenni (active

in Italian politics since before World War I and a Socialist since 1922), and closely allied to the Communist party, which controlled most of the joint labor, youth, women's, and other organizations. On the question of collaboration with the Communists the democratic Socialists, led by Saragat, seceded in 1947 and formed their own Social Democratic party. As the years went by, the position of the Italian democratic Socialists was clarified along the lines of northwestern European social-democratic and labor parties: they stood for free parliamentarian institutions; civil liberties; a welfare economy; and close collaboration with the United States within NATO, and with European democratic states within OEEC, the Council of Europe, and the Coal and Steel Community.

Soviet suppression of the Hungarian anti-Communist revolution in 1956 brought to a climax the tension that had been growing within the Socialist party since the early 1950's. The majority decided first to end the alliance with the Communists, later to follow the Social Democrats and to collaborate with the Catholics. The collaboration was to be on the basis of limited acceptance of the Catholic position in the fields of Church-state relations, supervision of communications media, education, and Western-oriented foreign policy; in exchange they were to receive Catholic support for a program of limited nationalization, agrarian reform, welfare measures, and economic planning. The clearly pro-Communist wing of the Socialist party seceded in 1963 and formed the Socialist Party of Proletarian Unity (or PSIUP). The outcome was that by 1964, although there were now four parties of Socialist origin (supported by about 45 per cent of the electorate), the three-way split within Italian socialism had been reduced to a two-way split. On one side were the Socialist party, with about four-fifths of the four and one-half million votes it had received in 1963, and the Social Democratic party, with two million votes. On the other were the Communist party, with eight million votes in 1963 and 1964, and the PSIUP, with the balance of the votes that had gone to the Socialist party in 1963.

With more than a million and a half members, the Communist party of Italy was all through the postwar period the largest in Western Europe. Despite its size, however, had it received no support other than that of a plurality of wage-earners it would have presented a comparatively unimportant problem. It was strong because of the fascination it held for a majority of the intelligentsia. Intellectual and professional people provided the brains, the organizing ability, and also that willingness to face sacrifices and hardships which is communism's main asset in non-Communist countries. In a nation where public life is characterized by a good deal of gross corruption and inefficiency, many non-Communists were impressed by the competence and honesty of local (municipal) administrations run by the Communist party. The socialism of most Italian Communist intellectuals is of the utopian variety. It implies an unshakable faith in the magic virtues of the final goal—integral collectivism. It combines the vision that inspired Saint-Simon and Fourier with the deep passion of Marx and the practical instructions of Lenin. It is a high-tension mixture of irrationalism and logic, of idealism and practicality. For the believers it is faith, with all the attributes of religion. Titoism, or national communism, has had little impact on Italian communism. But in 1964 internal cohesion was being weakened by the impact of the antagonism between the USSR and Red China, between Soviet Communists afraid of a major world conflict and followers of Mao who were not. Italian Communists' efforts to prevent a final break between Soviet and Chinese Communists were largely due to the desire to avoid a split within the Italian party. A pro-Chinese revolutionary party was organized in 1964. Khrushchev's defenestration in October 1964 was welcomed with relief by most responsible Italian Communists.

The one-sixth of the nation that in the early 1960's was neither Catholic (clerical, democratic, or leftist) nor Socialist (democratic or totalitarian) had little influence. The largest group in this section was that of non-Catholic conservatives, organized into the twin Liberal and Monarchist parties. Their main spokesman was the able parliamentarian Malagodi. In social and economic matters the position of non-Catholic conservatives was close to that of American right-wing Republicans. In external affairs they were staunch advocates of close ties with the United States, of the North Atlantic Treaty Organization, and of the European Economic Community. They opposed appeasement of communism in any form. The heirs to pre-fascist democratic parties, less numerous than the conservatives, supported the tiny but politically influential Republican party, led by the economist and statesman La Malfa. Lastly, there was the neo-Fascist Social Movement, supported by one citizen in twenty: enough to be a nuisance, not enough to be a threat. Neo-fascism was weakened in 1963 by a split between extremists nostalgically dreaming of the totalitarian state, and moderates willing to accept free democratic institutions for a time in the hope of one day being included in a rightist coalition with the Christian Democratic right wing and the non-Catholic conservatives.

At the time of writing, Italian democracy has the sincere support of five to six million democratic Socialists, of the Christian Democratic center (another five or six million voters), of the small Republican party, and of some non-Catholic conservatives. All together, this is a plurality only, though one large enough to remain in power as long as the agreement between democratic Catholics and democratic Socialists lasts. However, democracy is not the central problem for most Italians in the 1960's. The immediate future of the Italian nation largely depends on the capacity of Catholics and democratic Socialists, jointly or separately, to solve the internal and external problems that a majority of Italians consider more important than political institutions—the usual problems of economic security, prosperity, and peace at home and abroad.

International Relations

Internal political divisions are the key to Italy's external policies. Since the elimination of Communists from coalition governments in 1947, Italian foreign policy has for eighteen years followed a consistent line. Cooperation and friendship with the United States and its allies, and with Western European nations generally, have been the central motives of that policy. On the other hand, Italy may have been less deeply entrenched in the Western camp during this period than appeared to superficial observers, owing to the Communist movement's strength in the country and the appeal of neutralism to many non-Communists.

Italy was a charter member of the Organization for European Economic Cooperation, created in 1948, which played the fundamental role in European economic recovery and political stability in the 1950's, and which, with the addition of the United States and Canada, became in 1961 the Organization for Economic Cooperation and Development. Italy joined the Council of Europe, created in 1948. She was a participant in the negotiations leading in 1951 to the formation of the Coal and Steel Community which included Belgium, France, Italy, Luxembourg, the Netherlands, and West Germany. She took the lead in the treaties, signed in Rome in 1957, establishing the European Economic Community (called "The Six"). Cooperation with the other members of The Six was highly advantageous to Italian industry and labor. It created new outlets for Italian products and migration, it stimulated the expansion of the Italian economy. Within The Six Italy consistently advocated the enlargement of the Community and particularly the inclusion of Great Britain.

At the request of the United States government Italy joined the negotiations that led to the formation of the North Atlantic Treaty Organization (NATO). As a NATO member, Italy accepted American military bases on her territory. American funds contributed to the reorganization of Italy's armed forces, largely wiped out during World War II. (In 1964 the Italian military budget was about 4 per cent of the GNP, as against 11 per cent in the United States and 18 per cent in the Soviet Union. Italian armed forces included a well-trained and well-equipped army of more than a quarter of a million men and a small but efficient air force and navy.) The United States was generous in economic aid, from millions of CARE packages distributed freely at the end of World War II to the billion dollar loan granted in 1964 to bolster the Italian currency. On the Italian side, the government strongly supported American policies in all major crises: from the Berlin air-lift of 1948-49 and the Korean War of 1950-53, to the Berlin Wall crisis of 1961 and the Cuban crisis of 1962. She also gave her support in all questions concerning disarmament and nuclear control.

A member of the United Nations since 1955, Italy has taken an active part in all activities aimed at strengthening the organization and its specialized agencies. Although siding with the United States, Italian delegates tended to play a conciliatory role in crises affecting the United Nations, as when the Soviet Union opposed the then Secretary-General Hammarskjold, and later in the Yemen and Cyprus crises.

Radically reversing the aggressive policies of the Fascist period,

Italian governments did their best after the end of World War II to improve relations with countries near and far. It was not difficult to carry out this policy toward countries with which Italy had consistently been friendly, like the Latin American republics, Spain, and the United Arab Republic. It was more difficult to develop friendly relations with countries with which Italy had been at war, particularly those that during World War II had suffered considerably at her hands: Ethiopia, France, Greece, Yugoslavia. Even in these cases Italian diplomacy met with considerable success. Only with Austria were relations at times strained, because of the anti-Italian agitation of the German-speaking (Austrian) minority in the Alto Adige, before 1918 the Austrian South Tyrol. But even in this case tension never led to a break in diplomatic relations. Italy was particularly successful in establishing friendly contacts with newly independent states of the Middle East and Africa. Friendly contacts paid handsomely in greater opportunities for Italian trade, Italian investments, and Italian technicians.

Looking from the American side of the Atlantic, Italy, friendly with everyone, appeared strongly anchored to the United States-led system of alliances. But the chain holding the anchor was not as strong as it seemed. There was the large and efficient Communist party in Italy, a vehicle for Soviet influence. There was the growing appeal of neutralism to Italians of all classes. This was only secondarily the result of anti-Americanism; primarily it was caused by a desire to live in peace and to avoid dangerous involvements. Early in 1965 pro-Sovietism was not yet an alternative to the pro-American policies followed consistently by Italian governments since the spring of 1947, but neutralism was. Even in such a domestic affair as the choice of a new head of state, whose functions are largely ceremonial, the neutralism and anti-neutralism of the various candidates was a serious consideration. This happened in 1962 when lengthy political maneuvering preceded the election by Parliament of Segni as president of the republic. It happened with greater bitterness, leading to considerable tension that was close to jeopardizing the entire democratic structure, in December 1964 when Segni resigned because of illness. The neutralist wing of the Christian Democratic party, including about one-fourth of Catholic deputies, senators, and regional representatives, refused to vote for the official candidate of the party. Only after repeated balloting, considerations of internal policies prevailed over those of external policies, and the pro-American leader of the Socialdemocratic party, Saragat, was elected president of the republic with a two-thirds majority.

TWO

THE ROMAN HERITAGE

The Italian nation owes its birth to ancient Rome. It also owes concepts, values, and institutions which originated during the twelve hundred or so years of legendary and documented ancient Roman history. These underwent processes of revision, reinterpretation, and transformation but never disappeared.

From its origins, about which nothing is known with certainty, until the early third century B.C., Rome was just one of the hundreds of self-contained, highly diversified communities existing in the territory that is now Italy. The more advanced belonged to a variety of civilizations: Etruscan, Hellenic, Phoenician. But most had not gone beyond the stage of tribal organization: this was the case of Bruttii and Itali in the South, Ligures and Veneti in the North, of the better known Latini and Sabelli. There was no Italian people; instead, there were many peoples, differing racially and culturally. Centuries later, Rome was the vast Mediterranean state embracing much of Europe and North Africa, and parts of western Asia. Between the early and Mediterranean periods there was another phase during which Rome and Italy (at first the peninsula only, soon the continental north as well) were one. This was the birth-phase of the Italian nation. It lasted approximately from the second Punic war at the end of the third century B.C. until the final obliteration of the distinction between the ruler, Rome-Italy, and dependent territories, in the uniformity of the authoritarian Roman Empire in the third century A.D. Thirteen hundred years of political fragmentation during the Middle

Ages and in modern times failed to destroy the unity that Rome had achieved.

The Roman heritage is varied and complex. Much of it is part of Western civilization. But the elements that the Italian nation shares with others are more deeply marked in Italy than elsewhere. One element in the heritage is peculiar to the Italian nation, in the sense that in Italy it has acquired, at times, the status of a mass phenomenon. This element is the Roman imperial myth, which influences—sometimes obsessively—sectors of the educated classes, who see in Italy the legitimate successor of the ancient Roman state and long for a greatness that can no longer be attained.

Continuity

Even if the physical continuity of a people has been maintained, their past often is completely divorced from their present. An unbridgeable chasm may separate phases in the life of a community which ethnically has changed little. The ruins of Angkor and Borobudur, of Babylon and Byblos, are only historical curiosities for nations of southeast and western Asia. There is a gulf between Pharaonic and Arabized Egypt, between Mayan Indians and their descendants today in Guatemala and Yucatan. There is a gulf between Italians and the non-Roman cultures of ancient Italy. There is none between Roman and post-Roman Italy.

The abundant material evidence of the Roman past is not just an historical curiosity for Italians. They are still using roads and bridges built by ancient Romans. They worship and attend performances in what used to be Roman temples, lawcourts, theaters, and amphitheaters. Their language derives from the Latin spoken by the common people of ancient Rome. The imperial crown Frankish and Germanic leaders received in Italy from 800 to 1530 was the symbol of the continuity of the Roman idea. Roman offices and titles survived in post-Roman Italy. Heads of the administration governing Rome for centuries after the collapse of the Roman Empire were called patricians; so too were the members of oligarchies governing Italian republics in early modern times. Chief executives of the self-governing communities organized in parts of northern and central Italy in the eleventh and twelfth centuries were called consuls, and had functions similar to those of their predecessors. Pagan or Catholic, the head of the Roman and of the Italian priesthood was a pontiff. When twentieth century Fascists sought a title for their leader, they called him *duce*, from the Latin *dux*.

Material objects, language, and titles do not in themselves make the continuity. It exists, rather, because important elements of the Roman culture never entirely disappeared from the minds of post-Roman Italians. There have been fifty or so generations since the Roman state ceased to exist in Italy. There was no political unity from 568, when a new wave of invading Germans, the Lombards, failed to conquer the whole of Italy, until 1859-60, when a short war and a few successful raids and revolutions brought into being the modern united Italian state. An Italian consciousness overriding class and local loyalties does not appear until the development of Italian literature in the thirteenth century. During that long period Latin was the spoken and written language of the small educated minorities in Italy, giving them unity. More important, many of the books through which concepts and values were transmitted from generation to generation had Latin authors.

Until quite recently, the educated people of every generation in post-Roman Italy read the works of Cicero. Jurist, statesman, prolific writer, Cicero summarizes in clear, uncomplicated language the intellectual achievements and the political wisdom of the Roman world, deeply influenced (more so than Italians usually care to acknowledge) by Hellenic civilization. It was largely because of Cicero that in Italy the idea of a society founded on liberty, a republic in the Roman meaning of the word, never died. Through Caesar's autobiographical histories, the Roman expansion north of the Alps and the civil strife that caused the downfall of the republican form of government in Rome seemed to belong to a recent, not a remote, past. What Cicero and Caesar did for the first century B.C., authoritative Christian and Catholic writings did for the period of Roman decadence and collapse in Italy. Besides St. Paul (deeply conscious of being a Roman citizen), early Christian writers like Tertullian, Lactantius, and Ciprianus were Romans; so were the most influential Church Fathers, among them the two outstanding early systematizers of Catholicism, St. Augustine and St. Gregory Magnus. They were not just subjects of the Roman state, but Roman nationals brought up in the Roman culture. Their writings are full of references to the pre-Christian Rome which they sharply condemn. But they lived in the Roman environment and, in spite of the censure, it was through them that the environment remained alive for Italians.

Catholicism, the religion of most Italians since the disappearance of the Arian branch of Christianity in the seventh century, is impregnated with Roman concepts. Its medieval political antithesis, secularism, which appears in the twelfth century as the opposition in Catholic-dominated Italy, took its inspiration from Roman ideas and Roman experiences. Fourteenth and fifteenth century humanism was largely a reformulation of Roman (and Greek) concepts and values. Until recently Italian law was based on ancient Roman law. The histories of Livy, Sallust, Tacitus, and many other Romans, the works of Pliny and Marcus Aurelius, the poetry of Lucretius, Virgil, Horace, and a host of distinguished poets, the *Lives* of Plutarch translated into Latin, formed much of the syllabus in Italian education until at least the nineteenth century.

What Rome Was

To Italians, the Roman past has been a source of inspiration and at the same time a burden. This apparent contradiction stems from the fact that while many Italians, down to the Fascists of recent decades, wanted to emulate the achievements of ancient Rome, they lacked the qualities that had made for their ancestors' attainments. A brief excursion into the Roman past explains the difference between Roman and post-Roman Italians and the burden of an example which is admired but cannot be imitated.

The continuity between Rome and Italy and the impress left by Rome were primarily consequences of the slowness and steadiness of the internal and external developments of the Roman community: the slow pace at which its institutions grew and changed, and the slow regularity with which it expanded to become first the Italian state and later the Mediterranean empire. There is nothing unique in Rome's internal changes and external conquests; the uniqueness lies in the long duration of each development.

It took hundreds of years to build the way of life characteristic of the Roman community in its period of greatness spanning five centuries, from before 300 B.C. to after A.D. 200. We know what this way of life was when fairly reliable recorded history begins, early in the fourth century B.C. Legends have embellished and transformed the previous period, but whatever it was like, the Romans of the fourth century were already the end product of a process lasting several centuries. We know through documented history that it took more centuries to change that way of life to the point where it may be said to have been superseded by a new one. The new way of life, spiritually Christian, intellectually dogmatic, politically authoritarian, becomes dominant in the fourth century A.D. It had taken two generations to establish the republic; it took two generations to destroy it. Until bloody rioting broke out in 133 B.C., dissensions among the citizens had not led to any violence for over three hundred years. After the capture of Rome by Gauls around 390 B.C., eight hundred years elapsed before another enemy captured the city. It took nearly a hundred years (364-270 B.C.) of steady, sustained warfare, defensive at first and then offensive, to unify the Italian peninsula under Roman control. It took more than a hundred years of steady, sustained, aggressive warfare (264-146 B.C.) to make Rome the dominant Mediterranean power. It took nearly another three hundred years to make Rome the Mediterranean empire, and to transform a multitude of peoples into the Roman nation. It took a hundred years of continuous invasions, at a time when the Romans were undergoing a great spiritual crisis, to bring about the collapse of the Roman state in the West in the fifth century A.D. Weakened and shrunken, the Roman state in the East and its Byzantine successor lasted another thousand years.

One asks whether it is possible, in the web of forces acting in a society, to identify what made for this regularity, this steady gradualness and slowness, within the frame of what was for many centuries a free society of free citizens. The answer must be found among the intangibles which more than anything else make for a way of life: the dominant values giving direction to individual and collective behavior. Comparison between ancient Roman values and the values of present-day Italians mentioned in Chapter One, shows how different Romans and Italians are. What lasted were the achievements of ancient Rome, not what made the achievements possible.

Historians say that the fair and good life was the goal of the ancient Romans, or at least of the influential ones who patterned their lives on Athenian models. When Romans became Christians, they valued benevolence, humility, purity, together with obedience, patience, meekness. The Greek fair and good life appealed to a number of Romans, and at all times there were Romans who valued Christian virtues or their opposites. But what set the tone for the Roman community, and later for the Roman nation, was the presence of a large influential group who valued what the Romans called the virtues of the ancestors, and tried to reflect these in their conduct.

The writings of Latin authors are full of references to Roman values. Examples (many of course mythical) were held up to the younger generation. What the lives of the saints gave to Italians during the period of Catholic ascendancy was given to the Romans by the examples of Cocles, Scaevola, Torquatus; of the Horatii and the Fabian family; of the elderly senators who sat calmly in their chairs and without flinching let themselves be killed by the victorious Gauls; of Cincinnatus, Regulus, Virginius.

It is not difficult to identify some of the important Roman values. First came *virtus*, signifying manliness. In a military society, such as the Roman one remained for centuries, *virtus* meant primarily the behavior proper to a soldier: valor, indifference to death, discipline, obedience, initiative, sense of responsibility. With *virtus* went *constantia*, or endurance: fickleness, in any field of behavior, was despised. *Gravitas* meant not only that comportment should be dignified but also that life should be taken seriously. *Temperantia* was moderation and sobriety. Lucullus's gluttony, Crassus's greed, the sexual intemperance of Augustus' descendants and other family members, have become proverbial. But the behavior of a small minority, even an influential one, is not to be identified with the general behavior: had intemperance been dominant, Rome would not have lasted so long. *Fides* was the obligation to keep one's word, whatever the sacrifice involved; independently from legal sanctions, contracts were honored. *Pietas* was respect for elders, ancestors, parents, gods. Family cohesion was strong. The exalted position of the *paterfamilias* (humanized only toward the end of the Republic) has remained proverbial. The Roman woman, as spouse and mother, held higher status than women in other Mediterranean civilizations. All classes were religious, except, from the second century B.C., the Greek-oriented intellectuals. Rome was a nation of believers, not of worldlings

and agnostics, which turned to Christianity in the fourth century
A.D.: believers for whom traditional beliefs were no longer enough.

The Roman virtues amounted to a fairly harsh ethical code. Duty
prevailed over pleasure, self-sacrifice over personal gratification, self-
control over instinctive behavior. With such a code there could be,
and there was, cruelty both to self and others. Indifference to death
means also disregard for the lives of others. Those who submitted to
decimation (the execution of one soldier out of ten, if there had
been panic or fear) approved of large-scale crucifixions and gladiators'
games. In every generation there were of course Romans who were not
strong enough to stand the code, or did not approve of it. Beginning
in the second century B.C., and gradually becoming more and more
numerous, there were those who despised and hated it. But until at
least the third century A.D. enough Romans accepted the code to
give the Roman way of life its peculiar characteristics of steadiness,
regularity, and efficiency, envied by Italians in modern times.

Roman military success—key to the expansion of a community
which never excelled diplomatically or economically—was largely the
result of the ethical code. Romans were no braver than Samnites, Nu-
midians, or Gauls, for instance. Their military equipment was not
superior to that of Carthaginians, Macedonians, or Parthians (Rome's
main competitors in the Middle East). Roman generals were often
inferior to those of their opponents, to Pyrrhus, Hannibal, Mithri-
dates, and others, both civilized and barbarian. But the balance of
nearly five hundred years of offensive wars (from the time when the
Romans pursued the Gauls in central Italy, to Trajan's conquests north
of the Danube and in the Middle East) was in Rome's favor. Romans
were also successful in defensive wars in the west until the beginning
of the fifth century A.D., in the east much longer. Military organization, growing out of trial and error, of imagination and discipline,
was good. The result of training, discipline, and tradition was a rare
combination: the man who as a subordinate, from private to imperial legate, knew how to obey; who as a commander, of a squad or
of an army, knew how to lead. Militarily there is some resemblance
between Romans and both ancient Macedonians and modern Prussians, but the Romans had by far the longest career. The Macedonians' lasted less than two hundred years; the Prussians' less than
three hundred.

To conquer is one thing, to hold is another. The creation of a solid and lasting state was a major Roman achievement. This too was linked to the ethical code, particularly to the capacity for constant effort along definite lines. In the evolution of the state and the improvement of political institutions ancient Rome played an important role. For generations like ours, which take for granted bureaucratic organization, civil services, channels of authority, it is difficult to visualize what it meant to give efficient administration to a vast, populous, highly differentiated state. Previous large states (none as populous as Rome) had had rigid hierarchical structures. A small group (a caste in Egypt, a tribe in the ancient Persian Empire, a city in the short-lived Athenian empire) having the monopoly of physical force, of soldiers and weapons, ruled all other groups arbitrarily. Over a long period the Romans succeeded in building a complex, well-organized bureaucracy to take care of internal administration, security and order, protection against external attack, financial and economic problems, and public works.

The process of building such a bureaucratic structure began under the republic, but the results were not at first altogether satisfactory: too many offices were elective; there was no room for the civil servant as we understand him today. It was continued efficiently under the emperors. The bureaucratic foundation laid by Augustus was expanded and strengthened under his successors. The institutional structure was largely responsible for holding the Roman state together during the upheavals of the third and fourth centuries. It held the Eastern Roman Empire and its Byzantine successor together much longer. The revenue of the Roman state approximated one hundred million gold dollars during the early Empire; this figure seems insignificant today but it was a colossal sum in ancient times. Its collection, management, and disbursement required a large, competent fiscal bureaucracy. Diocletian's 116 provinces needed tens of thousands of officials and employees. A standing army of one-fourth to one-half million fighting men presupposed a complex, well-integrated command.

Local (municipal) administration was particularly important in republican and imperial times. Patterned at first on the Roman elective system, local administration of cities big and small, and of their rural areas, became more and more bureaucratic. There were executive boards, consultative councils, committees, elected officers, salaried permanent officials. When the central Roman administration collapsed in Italy in the fifth and sixth centuries, the municipalities survived (in Spain and North Africa until the Arab conquests of the seventh and eighth centuries, and longer in parts of Gaul). Records are scanty, but we know that municipalities functioned in Italy during the five hundred years of the early Middle Ages, and that their structure bore the Roman stamp. Distinct municipal territories, often corresponding to modern districts, can still be traced today. Cities declined but never disappeared, forming a link between ancient Roman civilization and the new Italian civilization of the second half of the Middle Ages.

The Roman Empire came and went. But the concern with the state and its proper structure remained, as did another creation of ancient Rome, Roman law. This, again, largely grew out of the ethical code, and it has deeply influenced the Italian nation, and many other nations, ever since. Roman law was developing slowly during the five hundred years between the unification of the Italian peninsula early in the third century B.C., and the beginning of the great turmoil and unrest of the third century A.D. Other ancient nations had the same deep sense of the law as the Romans, but the Romans created a new kind of law.

Communalism, and therefore conformity, prevailed over individualism in early Roman culture. For a long time the Roman community was largely impersonal, in the sense that the individual was completely subjected to general norms—customs, and those state-enforced customs called laws. The oldest Roman code of which we have knowledge, the fifth century B.C. laws of the Twelve Tables, was not essentially different from other ancient codes. The difference set in later. Romans were the first to divorce law from religion. This feat was as difficult as the divorce (achieved as yet only for a small section of mankind) of ethics from religion. No one can say why this should have happened in Rome and not elsewhere. However, it did happen and it opened a new road, not just in the field of legal relationships but in the much wider field of political activities and political organization. If laws are secular, they are man-made, and what man can make he can also change. The tradition sanctioned by a religious authority can give place to the sanction of the citizens. Reason—the ancient Ionian Greeks discovered—is what characterizes man; laws—added Roman jurists from the first century B.C. on—should be made according to reason.

To offset human fallibility the Romans stressed the importance of procedure, which is the best guarantee of the citizens' security. Individual will and arbitrary action are curbed in the measure in which procedure is paramount. The Romans moreover went further than any other ancient peoples in developing the concept of the person as an individual endowed with rights and duties. The person, as Roman jurists made clear, is the moral individual, just as the citizen is the political individual. The concept of the citizen, first developed by Romans, was basic to the enactment in modern times of the British and the American Bills of Rights, and of the French Declaration of Rights. The Romans went beyond their contemporaries in defining liberty, thus enabling future generations to conceive the autonomy of the individual as the foundation of self-government, or government by the people. They also went beyond in conceiving equality. Roman jurisprudence created the *jus gentium*, which is not the law of the states (as sometimes interpreted) but the law of the peoples. Roman jurists propounded moral and legal equality. In view of the particular development of Western economic systems, it was important that the Romans were the first to define in precise terms the concept of property. Ownership, contracts, obligations, and everything else pertaining to economic activities were carefully scrutinized and legislated by the Romans—as was also everything pertaining to the family.

Romans attached the greatest importance to the concept of justice (*justitia*). It was for them what charity has been for the Christians, what liberty was for English-speaking revolutionaries of the seventeenth and eighteenth centuries, what equality is for twentieth-century Socialists. The Romans were feared; they were also respected for their sense of justice. As long as people uncritically accept traditional positions sanctioned by religious belief, it is not difficult to decide what justice is. But once the need arises to define it rationally, as was the case for the new Roman secular law, what is it? The definition of justice formulated by Roman jurists and used in Roman courts is criticized today, but it was clear and it provided a sense of security: to give to each his due (*suum cuique tribuere*). This is the definition accepted ever since in most of the nations belonging to Western civilization. From it derives the effort to find out what rightfully belongs to each individual and each group. Romans legislated general norms, leaving to judges the latitude which in modern times has been a main feature of the British and American judiciaries. Because of the harshness inherent in the enforcement of general rules, Romans stressed fairness (*aequitas*).

Roman law was more than a set of legal norms. It had a philosophical foundation. It was closely associated with ethics. It had definite political and social corollaries. During the many centuries (down to a very recent past) when the study of law meant the study of everything concerning man in society, young Italians were trained in Roman law. The synthesis of Roman legal rules and jurisprudence compiled early in the sixth century by order of the Eastern Roman Emperor Justinian was for a long time the foundation of Italian law. Italian judges applied Roman legal procedure and, in spite of the vastly different environment, Roman principles of law. The authority of Roman jurists, of Gaius, Modestinus, Papinianus, Ulpianus, was quoted in legal discussions. The first Italian universities developed from the law schools in which Roman law was taught and interpreted.

Savoy
Piedmont

Swiss
Confederation

Tyrol

AUSTRIA

HUNGARY

Trent

Gorizia

Slavonia

Croatia

OTTOMAN

EMPIRE

FRANCE

Saluzzo

Asti
Mont ferrat

Mantua

Mirandola

Carpi

Massa
Bologna Faenza
San Marino Forlì

Rimini

Pesaro

Senigallia

Urbino
C.di Castello
Camerino
Perugia

Fermo

Ragusa

Monaco

Lucca

Florence

Piombino

Siena

Ligurian Sea

CORSICA

Papal States

Adriatic Sea

Sardinia

Tyrrhenian

Sea

Ionian

Sea

Mediterranean

Sicily

Sea

De facto independent states
Papal States
Aragonese (Spanish) Dominions

0   50   100   150 MILES

8° East of Greenwich   10°   12°   14°   16°   18° R.

MALTA
(to Sicily)

ITALY IN 1500

copy

THREE

THE MIDDLE AGES:
THE SHAPING OF
REGIONAL DIVERSITY

Historians have long debated the real nature of the Italian Middle Ages, and have disagreed about when this period began and ended. We do know that in the centuries immediately following the disintegration of the Roman state in the West two major developments took place that greatly influenced the Italian nation. One was the political fragmentation which led to the culturally sharp regional differences still important today, the topic of this chapter. The other was the ideological and institutional molding of Catholicism, the Italian version of Christianity and the central element of the Italian way of life, which is the topic of the next chapter.

There are two distinct phases in the fragmentation that took place during this period. The first is a time of decline, marked by wave after wave of invasions. During the second phase Italian states are independent, but what happens in the south is quite different from what happens in the north and center.

Foreign Invasions and Fragmentation

In the conventional view, the Roman state ended in Italy in A.D. 476. In that year Odoacer, leader of a motley collection of barbarian mercenaries (mainly Germanic Herulians), deposed sixteen-year-old Romulus Augustus, recognized as emperor the previous year. Nominally Odoacer was the representative of the Eastern Roman Emperor. In reality he ruled independently, and inefficiently.

What happened in 476 meant little to contemporaries. Roman (or,

41

rather, Graeco-Roman) civilization had lost its dominance in Italy and the rest of the Roman state during the fourth century. Through Diocletian's reforms, despotism, once hated and despised by Romans, became total. Constantine's victory in the civil war among Diocletian's successors was followed by the legal recognition of Christianity. State support facilitated the passage from a society in which religious pluralism prevailed to a society with one religion only. Dogmatism soon replaced what little critical thought remained. In intellectual as in political activities, authority and rigidity dominated. Economic activities were adversely affected by strict government controls. Farmers were becoming serfs. For several generations before the Vandals' invasion of 455, Germanic commanders of barbarian mercenaries were influential; after the invasion, they were in complete control.

In Italy the transition from the Roman way of life to one centered in Catholicism lasted about three hundred years, approximately from Diocletian's abdication (305) to the death of Rome's bishop, Pope Gregory I (604). By the end of this period territorial fragmentation had broken the unity achieved eight centuries earlier.

Dynastic conflicts, ambitions of Roman and foreign generals, and religious strife brought turmoil to Italy as to the rest of the Roman state in the fourth century. Conditions worsened: administration became less and less efficient, the economy declined, educational standards fell. Outside pressure mounted. In 376, the large Germanic tribe of the Visigoths (western Goths), fearful of the Mongolian Huns, crossed the lower Danube looking for protection in the Roman state. Instead of settling peacefully, they looted, destroyed, and killed in the Balkans until Arcadius, the Eastern Roman emperor, bribed them to cross into Italy. Defeated at Pollentia in 402, the Visigoths withdrew, to return shortly. In 410, led by Alaric, they occupied and looted Rome. For the people living then, it was the greatest disaster of all time, the end of the world. The Visigoths went from Italy to Spain where they ruled for three centuries, until the Arab conquest. This time Rome recovered, though not for long.

Political and religious conflicts continued in Italy. Other invaders arrived. The Huns spared Rome in 452, thanks to the entreaties of Pope Leo I, but ravaged much of the country. A deeper mark was left by the Vandals, who captured and looted Rome in 455. This time the city did not recover, and it was not long before its population fell to

50,000. Lacking maintenance, buildings became ruins, streets and squares disappeared. Odoacer was just one of many German tribal leaders who carved for themselves a state in Roman territory, and whose followers lived by exploiting the docile Christian Roman population. In 489, the Ostrogoths (eastern Goths) were led into Italy by their king, Theodoric II. Odoacer was defeated and the Herulians were never heard of again. With the Ostrogoths (489-554) Italy was still one state, but it was a state made up of two nations, each with its own political organization and culture. In 535 the Eastern Roman emperor Justinian I undertook the conquest of Italy. Ruthless war was fought for nineteen years. The defeated Ostrogoths disappeared from the scene of history. Italy, still one, was in ruins.

Justinian's success was short-lived. In 568 another Germanic tribe, the *Langobardi*, or Lombards, reached Italy. They occupied most of the north and half of the peninsula. The Roman Empire of the East, fast losing its Roman characteristics and becoming the Greek-speaking Byzantine Empire, kept the rest: an area astride Italy, including Rome, the Tiber valley, and the Exarchate (now Romagna) as far as the Po river; the islands and shores of the lagoons at the head of the Adriatic sea; the areas around the gulfs of Naples and Tarentum; the larger islands. Byzantine authority was uneven: weak in Rome, in the lagoon communities, in the cities on or near the gulf of Naples; stronger elsewhere. Italy was divided, and she remained divided until 1860.

Italy was transformed during these centuries. The population declined: in A.D. 600 it was probably no more than half of what it had been in A.D. 300. Many cities were abandoned, and in others lived only a fraction of the previous population. Public works and public buildings (except those being used as churches) were in ruins. Technical know-how deteriorated, trade shrank, poverty and ignorance prevailed. The new faith was creating a gulf between past and present which lasted several centuries. The Middle Ages had set in.

The decline continued for nearly five hundred years. Amid the chaos, however, a regrouping of Italian communities began. Except at times on the municipal level, what had remained of Roman administration under the Ostrogoths disappeared with the Lombards and the Byzantines. Conflicts among notables kept the Lombard kingdom of Italy in a state of tension, insecurity, and instability. A religious reform attempted in 726 by the East Roman or Byzantine Emperor caused strong resentment among his Italian subjects. Venice in the north and Naples and other cities in the south made themselves practically independent. They lived their separate lives, Venice until 1797, the others until 1860. The bishop of Rome, pressed by the Lombards and antagonistic to the Byzantines, asked the aid of the Frankish kings, then the most powerful rulers owing allegiance to Catholicism. In 756 Pepin III of France transferred to the bishops of Rome, the popes, the Byzantine holdings in central Italy. Confirmed by Pepin's son Charlemagne in 774, the transfer gave birth to what became known later as the papal states, which lasted, changed only slightly, until the events of 1859-70.

Frankish kings reigned for more than a century over what had been the Lombard state in Italy (except for two large duchies founded by Lombards in central and southern Italy). By the end of the ninth century, Frankish rule had become purely nominal, power being mostly in the hands of feudatories and ecclesiastical dignitaries. Some of the feudatories held the royal dignity (and nothing else) between 888 and 962, when the Saxon Otto I, already king in Germany, was crowned king of Italy and emperor. The Lombard, Frankish, and Saxon kingdom of Italy included most of the continental north and Tuscia (now Tuscany) in the peninsula. As time went on central authority in this kingdom became weaker and local communities were more and more on their own. In the tenth century, bishops and archbishops were first citizens if not actual rulers in many urban communities; nobles, mostly of Germanic origin, controlled rural communities; other communities governed themselves more or less democratically. Chaos, poverty, and ignorance were dominant.

The situation in the south was slightly, but not much, better. Moors (Arabized Berbers) expelled the Byzantines from Sicily in the ninth century, and held the island for over two hundred years. For a shorter time they held Sardinia and coastal areas of the peninsula. The southern half of the peninsula was divided into Byzantine possessions, maritime self-governing cities, and small states ruled by Lombard nobles who had made themselves independent of the kingdom in the north. Moral and material corruption were the mark of religious life everywhere in Italy, especially from the death of Pope Nicholas I in 867 until the rise of reforming influences in the eleventh century.

Italian coastal communities were in constant fear of raids by Moslem pirates from North Africa. Viking raiders appeared shortly after the middle of the ninth century. In the tenth century there were Magyar raids, as destructive as those of the Huns and Vandals five centuries earlier. The ninth and tenth centuries are the nadir of Italian culture.

Independence: The South

A new situation arose in Italy during the second half of the eleventh century. Or, rather, two new situations developed, one in the south, the other in the north and center. Results in the two areas were vastly different. The conventional description of the late Middle Ages in Italy is concerned mainly with what happened in the north and center—in the eleventh century, the regions included in a kingdom of Italy and in papal states that existed more in name than in fact. But for the Italian nation, then and now, what happened in the south was also important. In both cases, the change was primarily the outcome of action taken by the papacy, which was finally touched by the reforming zeal that had originated beyond the Alps in the tenth century. Freed for a while from moral and material corruption, the papacy was at that time guided for a third of a century by the clear will and firm hand of the Benedictine monk Hildebrand, adviser of popes before being pope himself (see Chapter Four).

Coexisting uneasily in the south at the middle of the eleventh century were three principalities still ruled by Lombards; several small maritime city-states, which had gained their independence or semi-independence from the Byzantine Empire in the eighth century and of which the most important politically and economically was Amalfi, south of Naples; Byzantine dependencies in Calabria and Apulia, exploited more than administered by military governors; and feuding Moslem emirates in Sicily. The island of Sardinia was going it alone: in 1018 the Moors had been expelled through the combined efforts of the two most important Italian cities on the Ligurian sea, Genoa and Pisa.

A few Frenchified Norman knights had been present as mercenaries in the South since the beginning of the century. Pilgrims to the Holy Land, they had stopped in conveniently located and relatively prosperous southern Italy, either on their way out or their way back, to pick up some badly needed money by fighting for one state or another.

A Norman knight became ruler of a minuscule state north of Naples in 1027. Another, William of Hauteville, was in 1043 created (by his employer, the Lombard duke of Salerno) Count of Malfi, a small inland city wrested from the Byzantines. William was the eldest of a large brood. Probably as many as ten of his brothers came to Italy, with their retinues of greedy squires and barefoot servants. Particularly able were Robert and Roger. In the best ninth century tradition of their Viking ancestors, the brothers raided, looted, and conquered. Hoping to escape destruction at the hands of the Norman adventurers, the citizens of Benevento put themselves under papal protection in 1052 (Benevento was a papal city until 1860 with few interruptions).

In 1059 Pope Nicholas II, advised by Hildebrand, decided to use the Hauteville brothers in bringing the Italian south under papal control by expelling schismatic Byzantines, infidel Moslems, and troublesome Lombards. Encouraged by papal blessing, and recognizing papal paramountcy, the Hauteville brothers did what was requested of them. By the time the job was completed early in the twelfth century, the Norman conquerors, now called Altavilla, were more Italian than French; they were not foreigners as countless conquerors had been before them. In name they were papal feudatories In reality they were independent rulers, and in spite of a nominal tribute the state they founded, the Two Sicilies, was an independent one. Repeated papal efforts to enforce paramount claims failed.

The Two Sicilies was nearly as large as the kingdom of England, conquered at about the same time by other Norman adventurers. It had, though, more than twice the population and several times the revenue. United or divided into its two main component parts—the Neapolitan kingdom on the mainland and the island of Sicily—independent or dependent, the state created by the Hautevilles lasted until 1860. It was Italian (this in fact was the time when Sicilians became integrated into the Italian nation), but it had its own distinctive variant of Italian culture. The story of the kingdom is the usual monotonous, sordid one of all despotic societies. In a long series of despots, a few are efficient administrators; under their rule comes a measure of economic progress and improvement in standards of living. Most are inefficient administrators and there is economic decline. A few are benevolent despots, and their tolerance makes possible the advancement of intellectual activities. Most are malevolent. On the

whole, in the eight centuries from 1059 to 1860, inefficiency and ma-
levolence predominate, as might be expected. The longer a dynasty
rules, the worse the internal situation becomes (happily for the
Italian south no dynasty lasted more than two centuries).

In the rare times when the state was ruled by a despot who was
both efficient and benevolent, there was intellectual and economic
flowering. Palermo, the Sicilian capital of the united kingdom for
over a hundred years, was the first seat of an Italian cultural revival
—in the twelfth century, when Roger II of Hauteville reigned, and
also in the thirteenth century, in the reign of the German Hohenstaufen Frederick II. What Palermo was briefly during those two
centuries, Naples, capital of the mainland Neapolitan kingdom, was,
also briefly, in the fourteenth century, when the Capetian Robert of
Anjou reigned, and in the fifteenth, under the Spaniard Alfonso of
Aragon. But in despotic societies golden ages are rare islands in oceans
of torpor and stagnation. Economic advancement and intellectual revival in southern Italy were just a series of widely separated short
flashes. In between there was decline: poverty and ignorance for the
masses, corruption in the upper classes, which included a large and
irresponsible nobility and a greedy, bigoted clergy. From the time of
Greek and Carthaginian colonization to the arrival of the Normans
the Italian south was more advanced than the north in every aspect.
Thanks to the centralized despotism introduced by the Normans and
continued by their German, French, and Spanish successors, the
South had become Italy's depressed area by the fourteenth century,
and has never recovered.

The united kingdom created by the Hautevilles in the south continued under their successors, the German Hohenstaufens and the
Capetian Charles I of Anjou. A conspiracy of nobles led to a successful popular revolt in Sicily in 1282. Peter III of Aragon (a kingdom in
northeastern Spain) was offered the crown of Sicily. The island was
an independent state under Aragonese princes until 1409. After that
date it kept its separate institutions, but for three centuries was governed first by Aragonese and later by Spanish viceroys. The long connection with Aragon and Spain deeply affected Sicilian culture and
the Sicilian way of life. Peter's son, James II, established Aragonese
rule over most of Sardinia in 1323-24. In the Neapolitan kingdom,
three times as large as Sicily, various branches of the Angevins re-

mained in power for over a century and a half. As the result of excessive misgovernment under the amorous Queen Joan II, of revolts, and of wars between pretenders supported by foreign states, another Aragonese, Alfonso V, became king of Naples in 1435. But Aragon and Naples remained separate for a while—as had Aragon and Sicily in the fourteenth century. In 1500 Ferdinand II, ruler together with his wife Isabella of most of the Iberian peninsula, signed a treaty with Louis XII of France for the partition of the Neapolitan state. A French land expedition late in 1501 and a Spanish sea expedition early in 1502 put an end to the independence of Naples for nearly two and a half centuries.

Independence: North and Center

Soon the South became a backwater, first culturally, then politically and economically. In northern and central Italy, instead, from the end of the eleventh to the beginning of the sixteenth century there was vigorous, if turbulent, progress. Achievements were great. When Hildebrand guided the papacy, most of northern Italy and Tuscany in central Italy were formally included in a kingdom ruled by the reforming Franconian Henry III (1039-1055), also emperor, king of Germany and Burgundy, paramount lord in Bohemia, Poland, and Hungary. French-invented feudalism was transplanted to this kingdom, chiefly by a process of imitation. In this hierarchical and well-integrated agrarian-military system, where relations between men were governed by their relationship to the soil, the top level was occupied by great lords, more numerous in Italy than north of the Alps. The dukes and marquises of Friuli, Ivrea, Montferrat, and Tuscany were particularly influential. Because of its agrarian nature, feudalism was incompetent to deal with urban communities where elected bodies often had the highest authority.

South of the kingdom of Italy were the papal states. Papal authority was effective only (and not always) in Rome and part of the surrounding area. In the papal states there was a sharp division between the country, where violent and ignorant nobles exploited the peasant serfs, and the cities.

In the northeast, independent from kingdom, empire, and papacy, was the Venetian republic. It did not extend much beyond the lagoon of Venice, but it had already acquired territorial holdings in the

Balkans. The sovereign body in Venice was a grand council including a fairly large percentage of citizens. A smaller council aided the chief executive, the *doge* (or duke), elected for life. The eleventh century Venetian republic was not democratic (as it had been in the early Middle Ages for several generations) but for the times, her citizens enjoyed an unusually large measure of political and economic liberty.

The political structure of the feudal kingdom of Italy at the middle of the eleventh century, and of the theocratic and largely nominal papal states (together embracing about three-fifths of all Italy), could be called loose. Then came almost complete political disruption. In the 1070's, the papacy clashed violently with the empire (see Chapter Four). Actually, since the Catholicization of what had been the Roman Empire in the West, there had been conflict between secular and ecclesiastical authority. For centuries both had been on the whole rather ineffective, and because this was the case, these clashes were fairly unimportant. Now both the empire and the papacy had been reorganized and strengthened, and the clash was correspondingly more violent.

The conflict between Gregory VII and his successors on one side, and the successors of Henry III on the other, was in reality, and particularly in Italy, a civil war. It meant an end to the fiction of a united European Catholic commonwealth, maintained since the time of Charlemagne. It meant the paralysis of government in the kingdom of Italy. There were excommunications of emperors by the popes and depositions of popes by the emperors. Who would owe allegiance to an excommunicated emperor-king, or to a deposed pope? As representatives and agents of imperial and papal authority, lords big and small, bishops, and abbots, lost their influence. If they had enough strength (in the basic political meaning of the term: military force) they could govern in their own right. But where temporal and spiritual lords were unable to enforce power, subjects became free to act on their own.

Thus it happened that at the end of the eleventh century and the beginning of the twelfth, urban communities of the kingdom of Italy were often left to themselves. They could without much risk expel imperial and papal legates and *vicari*. Citizens took the business of government into their own hands. The all-important development of the time was that citizens of the Italian cities, instead of looking for leaders and dictators (as people often do when they find themselves

suddenly free), organized parliaments, assemblies, and councils. They
elected their own officials, discussed their own problems, voted their
own laws. Moved by republican aspirations, they established republics
—as the term was understood at the time and had been understood in
ancient Rome. Even if limited and unevenly distributed, there was
a measure of political liberty, of government by the citizens. It was
the age of the *comuni*, communes—self-governing, politically organized urban communities.

In some cases records give the exact date of the organization of the
commune (for instance, 1135 in Florence and 1143 in Rome). In
many cases dates are uncertain. Among the earliest communes, functioning before the end of the eleventh century, were those of Genoa,
Lucca, Pisa, and—most important—Milan, the largest and wealthiest
city in the kingdom of Italy. The organization of a commune meant,
in practice, that neither imperial nor papal representatives any longer
exercized political and administrative authority. By the middle of the
twelfth century, most cities of the kingdom of Italy and of the papal
states had become *de facto* small, self-governing republics. This development was favored not only by the continuing feud between empire and papacy, but also by civil wars in Germany which weakened
the position of emperor-kings, and by Catholic schisms which weakened the position of popes.

The Concordat of Worms of 1122 between Emperor Henry V and
Pope Calixtus II failed to re-establish cooperation between secular
and ecclesiastical authority. During the civil war which followed the
death of Henry V emerged the factions called Ghibellines (from the
castle of Waiblingen in southern Germany) and Guelphs (from the
Bavarian Welf family, opponents of Lothair of Saxony and of Conrad
of Hohenstaufen). On the Italian scene, the Guelphs were those who
sided with the papacy, the Ghibellines with the emepror. Conrad's
able successor, Frederick I Barbarossa, tried to reassert the imperial
authority in the kingdom of Italy, where many cities had organized
themselves in anti-imperial leagues. Six times Barbarossa led powerful
expeditions south of the Alps. He destroyed the walls of Milan and
other cities. He occupied Rome. In addition to the wars between
Italians and imperials there were civil wars, because several Italian
cities, factions in anti-imperial cities, and many rural feudatories sided
with the emperor. In 1176 the soldier-citizens of communes allied in

the Lombard League inflicted a severe defeat on the imperial German knights at Legnano. Seven years later, at the peace of Constance of 1183, the emperor, who still called himself king of Italy, recognized the autonomy of the Italian communes. Local republicanism had triumphed. The process of territorial disintegration begun in 568 had reached its climax.

Independence did not mean peace, either externally or internally within each commune. Boundaries were often uncertain and communes were at odds with each other for the control of a village, a bridge, a few fields. There were jealousies, rivalries, ambitions. The more powerful communes tried to expand at the expense of the smaller ones. Feudatories in the rural areas looked greedily at the fast-growing wealth of the communes, and were a continual threat. Warfare was mostly on a small scale, but incessant. The conflict between neighboring Florence and Pisa, for instance, lasted until the beginning of the fifteenth century, when Pisa lost her independence.

There was little peace within the communes, either. The problem of peaceful coexistence in a state made up of citizens having different backgrounds, interests, and aspirations was as difficult to solve in medieval Bologna and Verona as it is in the United States today. At first, communes had a democratic foundation (always within narrow limits which excluded from the exercise of political power the inhabitants of rural areas and unskilled and poor city-dwellers). Citizens, often organized in their social orders or economic guilds and corporations, or a combination of both, formed a grand council, sometimes called parliament (from the Italian *parlare*, to speak). On the pattern of ancient republican Rome, the grand council elected consuls, the chief executives. The consuls' tenure was short and there was always more than one. An elected small council aided and advised the consuls. The scheme looked fine on paper. But, if Italians of northern and central Italy at the end of the eleventh century were mature enough to establish free self-governing communities, they were seldom mature enough to make liberty the permanent foundation of the independent city-states. Already at the end of the twelfth century, in many cities, the consuls began to be replaced by a *podestà*. The *podestà* had limited tenure, was often a professional man, and came from another city. It was hoped that as an outsider he could be a nonpartisan chief executive, and that factionalism would abate. To make discussions more manageable, grand councils were often reduced in size, or superseded by smaller councils.

The passage from the consular commune to the *comune podestarile* meant limitation, but not abolition, of political liberty. It was abolition, though, when a dominant faction, or the whole citizenry, called in a dictator, the *signore* or lord, to end violence caused by factionalism. This happened in Milan, for instance, even before the middle of the thirteenth century. The *signore* was often a member of the local rural nobility, still owning large tracts of agricultural land: Della Torre in Milan, Della Scala in Verona, Estes in Ferrara, Malatesta in Rimini, Pepoli in Bologna. Foreigners were sometimes asked to become *signori*: De Brienne in Florence, kings of France in Genoa. *Signori* were meant to hold power temporarily, but when free institutions have been suspended it is difficult to resurrect them. In the fourteenth century the transformation of *signori* into hereditary rulers became a general phenomenon. Once their position was confirmed by imperial or papal investiture and title, monarchical despotism was established.

The process described above does not apply everywhere. The Venetian republic found its internal peace in a closed oligarchic system formally established in 1297 (and which lasted until 1797). Attempts were made, by both Venetians and foreigners, to overthrow the oligarchy of the *Serenissima* (as the republic was called); they all failed. In Florence violent factionalism began in 1215 but republicanism survived for a long time. In their first period of ascendancy (1434-1494) the Florentine Medicis did what Augustus had done in ancient Rome: republican forms were preserved although the government was monarchical. In Genoa, no *signore* was ever able to become a prince. The tree of liberty planted in the eleventh century proved hard to kill. The Romans tried to re-establish their republic in 1347, the Milanese in 1447. The Florentines re-established their republican liberties twice, in 1494-1512 and 1527-1530. Through amalgamation, annexation, and conquest, the hundreds of independent city-states of the twelfth century were in 1500 reduced to two major states in northern Italy (the republic of Venice and duchy of Milan), and two in central Italy (the republic of Florence and the areas under effective papal control), and a score or so smaller ones.

FOUR

CATHOLICISM:
MEDIEVAL ORIGINS AND
CONTINUING ROLE

The post-Roman Italians of the long period of invasions and decline mentioned in the first section of Chapter Three can hardly be described as a nation. Still, there were bonds that served both to unite them and to differentiate them from foreigners and invaders. One, of course, was the Roman tradition, always meaningful in Italy. Another, even more important, was religion. Catholicism, originally the Italian version of Christianity, gave cohesion to the peoples of the continental north, of the peninsula, of the islands. Sicily, for instance, was not considered part of Italy either in ancient times or in the early Middle Ages; united politically during the first half of the twelfth century to the peninsular south, it became Italian because it was more Catholic than Orthodox.

Until the end of the thirteenth century, Catholicism was the dominant force in Italy, more important in molding the Italian way of life than native or foreign rulers, than force of arms or commercial pursuits. Ever since, although with considerable ups and downs, Catholicism has remained one of the major forces in the nation.

The pressures which during the last three generations have induced the Italian Catholic leadership (the upper echelons of the clergy and prominent laymen) to face, in fields other than the theological, the problem of change, originated outside Italy. They were the product of the general process of emancipation that characterized European nations shaken by the religious crisis of the sixteenth century and the

53

ensuing intellectual crisis of the seventeenth. Thanks to the loosening of authority, caused in Italy in the eighteenth century by conflicting imperialistic drives, these pressures appeared on the Italian scene through minority forces which achieved temporary success in the country in the nineteenth century (see Chapter Seven). In the tolerant and free atmosphere of the unified Italian Liberal state, Catholicism underwent a process of intellectual clarification and political reorganization. Since World War II, it has emerged as the dominant intellectual and political force in Italy. To understand today's Italian Catholicism and its pervasive influence on the nation, one must view it in relation to the long process of which it is the result.

The Italian Version of Christianity

The few centuries between the Christianization of Italians in the fourth century and the time of Pope Gregory I (590-604) constitute, theologically and intellectually, the main formative period of Catholicism. There had been a preparatory period during which Christians led a clandestine and dangerous life, a period common to Catholics and other Christians. Later there were important changes in Catholicism: in the eleventh and sixteenth centuries and again during the last hundred years. But until now changes have been an extension, never a negation, of early Catholicism.

The seven hundred years between the fourth and eleventh centuries were also the formative period, institutionally, of the Roman Church as an organization. Here again there have been changes, down to the recent greater autonomy granted bishops and archbishops, the increase in the number of cardinals, and various proposals made in 1962-64 at the Ecumenical Council Vatican II. Here too the changes have always aimed at greater cohesion and greater efficiency within the Church; they have not challenged the basic institution.

Catholicism was originally a specifically Italian movement, and it remained so for a considerable time. In Italy it acquired its chief characteristics. Except for relatively short periods, Italian influence continued to be paramount. The Church, centered in Rome and strongly impregnated with Roman elements, could appropriately be termed "Roman." The myth of the Roman Empire justified the adjective "catholic," or universal, at a time when Orthodox Christianity had a better claim to universality.

Military events in civil wars that had little or no connection with religion, but in which religious forces were useful pawns, enabled the Christian minority to triumph in the Roman state in the fourth century. Strengthened by secular authority, Christianity made rapid progress. Within two generations from the edicts of Constantine's early reign, Christianity held the allegiance of a majority of the population. The traditional Graeco-Roman anthropomorphic polytheism, Mithraism, and other Middle Eastern creeds centered in the worship of the forces of life (the sun, the mother-goddess), which had spread widely in the second and third centuries, lost ground and finally disappeared. So did Stoicism and Manichaeism, which once were widely diffused among the educated classes. As often happens, success bred divisions. The triumph of Christianity was accompanied by conflicts, by divergent interpretations of Christ's message and of the Scriptures, by organizational differences. The political division into two Roman Empires in the fourth century, and the disintegration of the Western one in the fifth, created autonomous sources of political power which in turn facilitated the rise of different Christian churches. Outside the Eastern and Western Roman states, Christianity assumed different theological and institutional features.

Each variation of Christianity felt the influence of earlier religious beliefs. At the level of intellectual formulation, each felt the influence of previously dominant philosophies. Organization was adjusted to different environments. All this—beliefs, philosophies, organization— made for the distinction between what came to be known as the Orthodox Christianity of the East Roman or Byzantine Empire, and the Catholic Christianity of Italy. It also gave distinctive features to Nestorian Christianity in the Middle East, Coptic Christianity in Ethiopia, and the Christianity of Ireland in the early Middle Ages.

Italian Christianity began to acquire its own characteristics in the fourth century, when the Italian Christian clergy sided unequivocally with Athanasius in his quarrel with Arius. The ecumenical council held in Nicea condemned Arius in 325. However, for a while Arius' theses prevailed in the East Roman Empire, and most Germanic tribes, on becoming converted to Christianity in the fifth century, chose Arianism. The Athanasian concept of the Trinity is fundamental to Catholicism and to most of Protestantism. The Athanasian stress on celebacy gave the regular and secular Catholic clergy its specific character and contributed to the influence it exercised. Athanasius' emphasis on asceticism promoted the growth of monastic orders, among which the first and for many centuries the most important was the Catholic Benedictine order, founded in the first half of the sixth century by an Italian, St. Benedict. In Italy developed the Petrine principle, according to which the bishop of Rome, as successor to St. Peter, is not first among peers but bishop of bishops. The primacy of the see of Rome was accepted, although still in a restricted sense, by a council of bishops of the Western Roman Empire held in Arles in 314. Through his quarrel with Emperor Theodosius in 390, St. Ambrose, bishop of Milan, established the principle of the superiority of ecclesiastical over secular power—while in the East Roman Empire the ecclesiastical authority was subject to the state. St. Augustine's concept of sin and redemption, together with his refutations of Manichaeism outside Christianity, and of Donatism and Pelagianism within Christianity, were among the pillars of Catholic doctrine.

In St. Augustine, as in Athanasius, Catholics and most Protestants have a common ancestor. The case of Gregory the Great is different. St. Gregory, the Roman patrician who was elected bishop of Rome and as such was pope from 590 to 604, the intellectual who hated Graeco-Roman thought, the man of culture who wanted to eliminate what remained of pre-Christian civilization, the prolific and powerful writer, contributed perhaps more than anyone else to the distinctiveness of Catholicism. The ideals to which he devoted his life and untiring energy were the ascendancy of the Roman ecclesiastical hierarchy, the uniformity of the ritual, the predominance of the Catholic dogma. Catholic liturgy is largely the liturgy of St. Gregory (even if the Gregorian chant did not originate during his pontificate).

St. Gregory's many written works occupy a foremost place among authoritative Catholic writings. Together with the works of other Church Fathers, with decisions of ecumenical councils, and, in recent centuries, with papal pronouncements, they are for Catholics on a level with the Scriptures. Adjusting the Bible to the intellectual and practical requirements of different times through free allegorical interpretation, St. Gregory's writings have contributed to the formulation of the distinctive Catholic theology—radically different from that of Christians for whom the Bible is the only authoritative source. A Christianity dedicated to the care of souls of the departed, praying to the Virgin and the saints as intermediaries between man and God, peopling the extraterritorial life with angels and demons (whose hierarchical order is reminiscent of man's classes and castes) appealed to Italians whose Roman forebears had honored the souls of their ancestors, worshipped deities, and felt the fascination of Eastern mother-goddess creeds. Although St. Gregory was repelled by Graeco-Roman civilization, he did more than anyone else to facilitate the absorption of pagan residues into Italian Christianity, and whatever paganism hostile to Christianity had remained in Italian communities disappeared. A Benedictine monk himself, St. Gregory promoted the monastic life in Italy. He was responsible for the consolidation of Catholicism in Italy through the conversion of the Lombards, who had previously embraced Christianity in its Arian interpretation. St. Gregory also promoted the spreading of Catholicism outside Italy by way of missionary activities in southern Germany and in Great Britain.

More important in terms of long-range cultural developments than for the masses of believers was the formulation of the Catholic conceptual framework. By means of the role played by reason in Catholic thinking, Catholicism sets itself apart from previous and contemporary religions: its philosophy is as distinctive as its theology. Like all other religions Catholicism is founded on intuition, the immediate apprehension of the truth. Supernatural beliefs are accepted through an act of faith (and can be accepted only in this way). But what in other religions, or in the most important of them, was the whole, in Catholicism was only a part, even if a large part. Catholic thinkers have not been satisfied with making statements. They have always been concerned with explanation and justification. This has meant the use of the rational process as well as intuition.

It was not enough, during Catholicism's formative period, to state that Manichaeism was a negation of Christianity. The statement had to be demonstrated. It was not enough to state that non-Catholic versions of Christianity were errors. This had to be proved. For centuries Catholic writers labored to demonstrate the validity of their beliefs. Dogmas and all kinds of obstacles, including fear and the pressure of conformity, limited the field within which reason could be used. Methods synthesized in the scholastic formulation were largely sterile as far as the development of new concepts was concerned. Certainly there was no free inquiry in Italy until Catholicism weakened and lost its political grip. There was little scope for the scientific method. But, within limits, reason was conceded an important role. Logic, the discipline concerned with the study of the proper use of reason, retained a distinguished place in formal education. Mysticism was usually discouraged among Italian Catholics, more so for instance than among the Greek Orthodox.

Because it recognized the role of the rational process, Catholicism became the channel through which was saved the greatest single feature of Graeco-Roman civilization: the conscious use of reason. Not all was saved of the Ancients' philosophical achievements, but enough to provide the foundation for the revival of rationalism, and therefore for the progress of scientific thought in modern times. Christian writers of the second and third centuries whose works were accepted as authoritative by Catholics, authors like Tertullian and Cyprian, had been reared in the Graeco-Roman philosophical tradition. The members of the great triad of the fourth and the early fifth century—St. Jerome, St. Ambrose, and St. Augustine—were highly cultivated people, cognizant of Graeco-Roman rationalism in several of its interpretations. Through them and others survived elements of Platonism, neo-Platonism, and stoicism, and the empirical reasonableness of Cicero. Aristotelian thought faded, but it reappeared in Italy in the twelfth and the thirteenth century, to be incorporated in the Catholic conceptual framework. Without Italian Catholicism the awareness of reason might have been buried under the ruins of the Western Roman Empire, and under the political and intellectual totalitarianism of the East Roman Empire.

St. Thomas Aquinas, born in central Italy not far from Rome, wrote his great philosophical synthesis toward the middle of the thirteenth century. He enriched and modified Catholic thought by grafting Aristotelianism onto scholasticism. What St. Gregory means to Catholic theology, St. Thomas means to Catholic philosophy. In the modified and modernized form of neo-Thomism, that synthesis is still valid for Catholics, and it is fundamental to the intellectual training of educated Catholics. Where rationalism is concerned, St. Thomas was not an innovator. He was simply a milestone in the long road beginning in the early times of Catholicism. The Ancients owed their intellectual achievements, and the Moderns owe their progress, to the awareness of reason. It made for the intellectual revolution which, through scientific discoveries, led to the technological inventions that have transformed human life. In spite of its detestation of the Graeco-Roman civilization, Italian Catholicism was the link between Ancients and Moderns.

The Institutional Frame of Catholicism

Catholicism developed unique features in another field, that of institutions. From the standpoint of practical or political activities, and so of power relationships, these institutional features are more important than theological dogmas or philosophical theses. If Catholicism is today a major force shaping the destiny of man, it owes its strength and influence in part to the number of believing Catholics, but more to the disciplined and efficient cohesiveness of the Roman Catholic Church, the result of the organizational structure.

The growth of Catholic institutions was a slow process that went on for centuries. They were developed in Italy, and influenced by the conditions prevailing between the fifth and eleventh centuries. The result was a centralized, hierarchical structure in which power, rigidly determined and circumscribed, descends from the higher to the lower echelons; and in which careful screening accompanies the passage of any individual from a lower to a higher level of authority. In spite of the pre-eminent position of the pontiff, Catholicism is best described, organizationally, as a closed oligarchy. The chief characteristic of such a system is that no one can join the oligarchy, at any level, without the approval of those who are already members. The closed oligarchy is the formula that best guarantees the continuity and stability of any organization. The Spartan state in ancient Greece, and the Venetian republic down to the end of the eighteenth century, were, on a small scale, good examples of closed oligarchies. They were spared much of the turmoil and fluctuation caused by popular emotions in democracies (and also, to some extent, in open oligarchies), and by the individual traits of rulers in despotic monarchies.

The organization of early Christian communities in Italy did not differ from that of others in the Roman state. During the centuries when Christianity was mainly a clandestine and persecuted movement, each congregation was organized along democratic lines and enjoyed a good deal of autonomy. The members of the congregation elected their pastor, who was not necessarily an ordained priest. In important cities, congregations elected the bishop. A council of elders was entrusted with administrative functions. Relations between congregations were on an equal associative basis. But hierarchical features appeared early. They were already implicit in the way priests were ordained. They were strengthened by the exalted position achieved by priests in some churches (often as the result of outstanding personal qualities), as necessary intermediaries between the faithful on earth and the heavenly host surrounding God. Moreover, pastors of congregations in important cities enjoyed greater prestige and influence than others. These factors were particularly important in Italy, and in the Western Roman Empire generally. Even after the city ceased to be a capital (in 330), the myth of Rome was strong in Italy; as no city could compare with it, so no bishop could have as much authority as the bishop of Rome.

Most important for the institutional growth of Catholicism was the political disintegration of the fifth century. It left a void, a power vacuum, which was filled by religious leaders. It would be wrong to assume that in this century and those immediately following, priests and monks, bishops and—later—abbots looked for political power. Perhaps some did, but not many. Political power came to them because there was no one else to take it. What happened in 452 when the bishop faced conquering invaders as leader of the entire population of Rome, was now happening in many other Italian communities. In the East Roman Empire, government authorities could effectively protect the people most of the time, or at least try to do so. By the same token they could also control the ecclesiastical organization.

In Italy, and in many other areas of what had been the Western Roman Empire, when people were threatened by invaders (as was too often the case) or even by internal disorder, they had only their religious leaders to turn to for protection. The Ostrogoth kings held little effective authority; the later Lombard, Frankish, Italian, and German kings in the north, and the motley collection of Byzantine governors, and Lombard dukes and counts in the south, had still less. Instead of the complex and efficient bureaucracy of the first four centuries of our era, there were only rudimentary, incompetent administrations. In the eighth, ninth, and tenth centuries there were governments competent to fulfill the basic function of efficiently guaranteeing the security of the people in only a few small city-states like Venice and Amalfi, and in Sicily, which was ruled by Moslem emirs.

It is not surprising that under these conditions the influence of the clergy extended beyond questions of faith and morals; that ecclesiastical authority became more and more impregnated with political power; that the authority of bishops and abbots increased; that the greatest authority was held by the bishop of Rome, the pope. What was done institutionally, from the time of the triumph of Christianity in Italy to the time of Gregory VII in the second half of the eleventh century, was simply to formalize an existing situation. That the Church became a political body with a rigid authoritarian hierarchical structure was the response, in Italy, to the chaos of the times and the accompanying insecurity. This remained a permanent feature of Catholicism.

The elective element first weakened and then disappeared. Bishops, from being simple supervisors, became heads of the clergy. The bishop of Rome became the head of the bishops. In the institutional field, Hildebrand of Soana (Pope Gregory VII) occupies the position that Gregory the Great occupies in the theological field, and St. Thomas in the philosophical. Hildebrand, born around 1015, was a Tuscan from central Italy, not far from Rome. Unlike Gregory the Great and Thomas Aquinas, he was of humble parentage and did not achieve distinction as a writer. Action was the whole focus of his life. Already as a young man he felt the strong appeal of the Catholic reform movement, which had started in eastern France and western Germany early in the tenth century, reaching Italy several generations later. The Burgundian monastery of Cluny, the leading center of reform and religious zeal, was his spiritual home.

In 1046 three clerics were quarreling, each claiming to be invested with the papal dignity. Hildebrand was in attendance on one of them. When in 1049 the German bishop of Toul (in Lorraine, at that time a duchy of the German kingdom) was chosen pope, he brought Hildebrand with him. For thirty-six years, Hildebrand was the highest authority and the greatest influence in the Church—first as adviser to popes, then as pope himself for twelve years, until his death in

1085. All of his action was based on three principles: the purity of the clergy, the supremacy of the papacy in the Catholic Church, the supremacy of the church over the state. He had on his side the growing number of Catholics convinced of the necessity for reform. He also had on his side, for political reasons, a majority of responsible Italians. His main enemies were the dissolute sector of the Catholic clergy, the German kings and emperors of the renewed Roman Empire who wanted to subordinate the church to the state, and the Byzantine Empire (still holding areas of peninsular Italy) as protector of Orthodox Christianity.

Hildebrand was largely responsible for the Lateran Synod of 1059, where decisions were taken that have remained fundamental for Catholics ever since. Laymen were deprived of what voice they still had in Church affairs. The celibacy of the clergy became an absolute rule, strengthening their moral position and widening the gulf which in the Roman Church separates them from the laity. The clergy became more and more an ecclesiastical bureaucracy subordinated to the popes. Popular election and imperial confirmation were eliminated in the election of popes. The papal electoral college was limited to the cardinals, the pastors of major churches in Rome and its suburbs, who in turn were appointed by the pope as bishop of Rome. National Catholic churches were deprived of their autonomy, and brought under the obedience to Rome. In 1075, as pope, Gregory VII issued the *Dictatus Papae* which stated in unequivocal terms that the emperor and all other temporal rulers were subordinate to the papacy, which could deprive them of their authority just as it could deprive the bishops of theirs.

The reorganization of the Catholic Church and the consolidation of papal authority had important results in the relationships between Catholicism and Orthodox Christianity. In addition to stimulating the Crusades, which started at the end of the eleventh century, they also had a deep impact on Italian political developments. Where Orthodox Christianity was concerned, *de facto* separation had existed for centuries, but an attempt had always been made to maintain the fiction of Christian unity between the two major Christian churches. There were theological differences and, more important, institutional differences. Aware of the dominant trends in Catholicism at the middle of the eleventh century, the patriarch of Constantinople, the highest ecclesiastical dignitary in the Byzantine Empire, definitely and finally broke all relations with Catholicism in 1054-1056 (a few years before the Lateran Synod). Subsequent efforts to re-establish cooperation, or at least concord, failed. (These efforts have been renewed now.) The 1056 schism had immediate repercussions in Italy (see the second section of Chapter Three); the papacy encouraged Norman adventurers to unify southern Italy.

The schism of 1056 and the unification of the south were important for Italy. No less important was the clash of the papacy with the Western Empire (later the Holy Roman Empire), revived a second time in 962 when the Saxon Otto I, king of Germany since 936, was crowned emperor and king of Italy. The clash was a major factor in the transformation of the kingdom of Italy and the papal states at the end of the eleventh century and during the twelfth century (see the third section of Chapter Three, and Chapter Five).

Who had precedence, emperor or pope? As long as the Church lacked an effective central authority and as long as the papacy was weak and corrupt, the answer did not matter. Nor did it matter as long as the imperial dignity lacked content, as it did under Charlemagne's successors. But then the empire was reorganized. And three generations later, under Hildebrand's strong leadership, the papacy too was reorganized. It was fortunate for the advocates of Church supremacy and of papal leadership that Emperor Henry III died in 1056, leaving a six-year-old heir and the conflicts and weaknesses that often accompany a regency.

The situation changed when young Henry IV came of age. He strongly resented the *Dictatus*. Also, a practical question was becoming more and more acute. Many clerics in the kingdoms of Italy, Burgundy, and Germany forming the new Roman Empire held both ecclesiastical and secular power—the care of bodies was joined to the care of souls. The bishop in charge of a diocese was, for instance, also a count in charge of secular administration, a cog in the complex feudal system. Who was to appoint the bishop-count? On this question arose the investiture struggle, basically a struggle between church and state. It started in 1075, when a synod called by Gregory VII in Rome passed a severe decree against the lay, i.e. imperial, investiture of clerics. Henry IV answered with the Synod of Worms, which deposed the pope, whereupon Gregory VII excommunicated the emperor. In and outside Italy most of the clergy and laity sided with the pope. In 1077 Henry IV made penance and at Canossa asked the pope's forgiveness.

This was only the beginning of a generations-long duel between papacy and empire. The duel was a major factor in the disintegration of imperial authority, first in Italy and later—in the thirteenth century—in Germany. It was also a major factor in the decline of papal authority in the fourteenth century, in Italy and elsewhere. The papal-imperial duel having annulled imperial authority in the kingdom of Italy, and the papacy being incapable of imposing its authority, one result was liberty for local communities in the north, in Tuscany and in most of the papal states.

Crises and Slow Change

The institutional rigidity attained by the second half of the eleventh century—fruit of efficient hierarchical authoritarianism—gave Catholicism the continuity and stability that have characterized it ever since. The same institutional rigidity put a brake on change caused by the pressure of internal forces. In the last nine hundred years Catholicism in Italy has gone through phases of flowering and decline, of fervor and indifference, of spiritual zeal and material preoccupation, of power and weakness. It has withstood all crises. As a creed and as an organization it has remained essentially unchanged. Attempts were made, from the inside, to transform it: from the evangelical and conciliar movements of the twelfth and fifteenth centuries to Jansenism and modernism in more recent times. The attempts failed. The survivors among those who wanted radical theological and institutional changes in Catholicism had to leave the Church. This usually meant exile, or ostracism if they remained in Italy. What limited changes did take place were largely the result of pressures by forces external to the Catholic Church and to Italy.

The Cluniac-inspired period of Gregorian reforms was succeeded by the twelfth century "age of faith" of history textbooks—an age which declined in the thirteenth century and faded away in the fourteenth. It was the age of papal supremacy and of great political popes like Alexander III and Innocent III, the latter convinced that he had finally achieved the unity of the Catholic Commonwealth under the supreme leadership of the papacy. Then lived great Catholic saints and scholars. New monastic orders were founded. Magnificent cathedrals were erected. Scholastic logicians wrote and taught. The Thomistic philosophy was formulated. It was also the age of crusades against Moslems in the Middle East, against pagans in northeastern Europe, against non-Catholic Christians in France and Italy; and of victorious wars against Iberian Moslems.

This was the age in which Catholic intolerance became organized. The combination of religious zeal and strong centralized organization made it more effective than the intolerance of other Christian churches and non-Christian religions. The crusaders were cruel not only to Moslems but to all non-Catholics. Gregory VII had already been set on eliminating the evangelical Patarines. Now the Catari were completely destroyed and the few surviving Waldensians who escaped the crusaders' swords fled to the Italian Alps. The term "inquisitor" was first used in 1163, when Alexander III was pope. Under Innocent III, who became pope in 1198, and his immediate successors, the Inquisition was systematized. Inquisitors condemned: the state—the secular arm—carried out the executions. The Inquisition went through periods of greater or lesser activity, according to the strength or weakness of the Church in relation to other forces. In Italy, it functioned effectively until checked by the tidal wave of religious and intellectual revolutions which culminated in the political upheaval at the end of the eighteenth century. Arnold of Brescia, Stabili, Savonarola, Carnesecchi, and Bruno were some of the illustrious victims who died. The most eminent of those who survived was Galileo. The voices of the sixteenth century Socinis of Siena, who stood for tolerance as a Christian virtue, were silenced. No Italian believers echoed the views on tolerance of Roger Williams, George Fox, John Locke. In Italy, religious tolerance, in the fourteenth as in the nineteenth century, was an anti-Catholic slogan. (And in 1964, three American cardinals who asked for the recognition of religious liberty by Catholicism were opposed by the Italian Catholic leaders.)

The post-Gregorian phase of papal ascendency ended in 1303, when an officer sent by the king of France arrested Pope Boniface VIII. For the next two and a half centuries, a church which seemed to have lost its faith was held together mainly by its institutional frame. All Italians were Catholics, but few of the educated people believed, while for the masses religious belief bordered on superstition, religious

ritual on magic. Chaos in the papal states induced popes and cardinals to live in comfort and security at Avignon, in southern France,
for two generations. Personal rivalries led to schisms which lasted
forty years more. An attempt, during the first half of the fifteenth
century, to replace papal with conciliar leadership failed. After the
schisms ended, a dozen or so popes were more concerned with politics, letters, and arts than with faith. The chief preoccupation of many
was to create in Italy a secular state for their sons or nephews: the
Borgia pope failed, the Cybo, Della Rovere, Medici, and Farnese
popes were successful.

Then came the storm. At first, few members of the Italian Catholic
hierarchy, from the popes down, paid attention to Luther's ninety-
five theses nailed on the door of Wittenberg's cathedral in October
1517. Few, if any, heard of Zwingli in Zurich, of Farel in Geneva.
But in Germany in the late 1520's and early 1530's the revolts of the
Anabaptists in Thuringia and Westphalia, Melanchthon's presenta-
tion of the Augsburg Confession, and the Schmalkaldic League and
the war it waged had serious political implications. Henry VIII's Act
of Supremacy, the final chapter in a conflict between the king of
England and the pope which had lasted several years, was also serious.

Pope Paul III (1534-1549) was primarily concerned with the political fortunes of his family, but around him were people now wor-
ried about what was happening beyond the Alps, and beginning to
happen in Italy. In 1536 Paul III created a commission to study the
situation: it became the battleground for two parties. On one side,
led mainly by the Italian Contarini and the Englishman Pole, were
those favorable to theological and institutional changes that would
make possible an agreement with the Protestants. On the other side,
led by the Italian Caraffa and vigorously supported by the Spaniards
Loyola, Laynez and Salmerón, were those who rejected all compromise, wanted to maintain the theological and institutional structure of
the Catholic Church intact, and aimed simply at making authoritarianism and centralism more efficient through greater discipline of the
clergy. Contarini, spokesman for the *conciliatoristi* (moderates), met
Melanchthon at Regensburg in 1541; the agreement he reached was
rejected in Rome. The *rigoristi*, as the intransigents were called, had
the upper hand, and the Counter Reformation was on.

The Roman Inquisition (distinct from the earlier papal Inquisition) was reorganized in 1542. In 1543 it was decreed that no book could be published without approval of ecclesiastical authorities. Various lists of forbidden books were consolidated in the *Index* of 1559, made more complete in 1564. Paul III was succeeded by leaders of the *rigoristi*. Their work as efficient inquisitors later brought Ghislieri, Peretti, and Aldobrandini to the papal throne. The Council of Trent met in 1545 to deal with the situation created by the Protestant reformers. Interrupted several times, it drafted the *Professio Fidei Tridentinae*, which received papal sanction in November 1564. The doctrinal line was, by and large, that of the Jesuit order, founded by Spaniards in 1534, approved by the papacy in 1540. The council, however, was mainly an Italian affair. (For instance, in the later sessions there were 189 Italian bishops and only eighty-one non-Italian.) Ever since, the *Professio* has remained the foundation of Catholic doctrine and institutional structure. The catechism taught to Catholic children in Italy is based on it.

The Council of Trent (nineteenth ecumenical council) explicitly put Catholic tradition on a level with the Scriptures; reserved to the clergy the sole right to interpret the Scriptures; stressed the essential importance of the seven sacraments and therefore the more than human character of the priest who administers them; and confirmed the dogma of transubstantiation, the cult of relics and images, the doctrine of salvation through both works and faith. The council closed questions previously left open, and recovered for papal authority what had been lost since the time of Boniface VIII.

As had happened in the twelfth century—but now with more purposeful and better organization—there was, during the second half of the sixteenth century, a revival of religious zeal in Italy. There were many canonizations. Catholic educational and charitable institutions multiplied. Corruption ended among the clergy, or at least for the most part. New religious orders were established, missionary activities intensified. At a time when Italians were becoming poorer, economic suffering was mitigated by increased charitable work. There was greater concern for the poor, the sick, the aged, for widows and orphans than ever before. At a time when the English and Scots, French, Dutch, and others were disturbed by new ideas and torn by dissensions,

Italians (except for a few) enjoyed spiritual calm, intellectual peace, and—for the most part—political order. These benefits they owed to the Counter Reformation.

Formally, the Church in Italy still represents the Catholicism that issued from the Council of Trent. But is this the case below the surface? No definite answer can be given. Non-Catholic forces operating in all fields of human endeavor have put pressures on the Church which may well lead to fundamental changes. The 1540 conflict between *conciliatoristi* and *rigoristi* (moderate innovators and rigid traditionalists) has been revived in recent decades. The conflict is more evident outside Italy, and it usually follows national lines (with Irish Catholicism, for instance, holding positions different from those of French Catholicism).

None of the important non-Catholic pressures influencing Catholicism originated in Italy. They gathered strength outside the Catholic world. Most—from free-thinking to existentialism, from liberalism to democracy and socialism, from nationalism to internationalism—had a common denominator: liberty, or the aspiration toward liberty. Violent political changes destroyed, or at least weakened, the close connection between Church and state realized in Italy at the time of the Council of Trent. It happened to some degree when Austrian armies took over parts of Italy during the first half of the eighteenth century; more so when French armies overran Italy at the close of the same century. New ideas and values coming from France and Great Britain, and later from Germany as well, spread widely among the Italians. The unification of Italy in the nineteenth century left Catholicism surrounded by hostile intellectual and political forces. It was on the defensive. As a power for molding the life of the nation, it reached its nadir in the second half of the nineteenth century. The trend has been reversed since the end of World War II—thanks largely to the earlier patient efforts of responsible religious and lay Catholic leaders.

The clarification of doctrinal positions had, as its major steps, the encyclicals *Mirari Vos* of 1832, *Quanta Cura* of 1864 (with its appendix, the *Syllabus Errorum*), *Aeterni Patri* of 1879, and *Pascendi Gregis* of 1907. The first condemned intellectual and spiritual liberty as universal principles—valid for Catholics and non-Catholics alike. The second made a complete list of philosophical, theological, and political errors; affirmed the complete independence of the Catholic Church from state control; claimed for the Church control over education, culture, and science; and rejected the idea of tolerance. The third confirmed Thomism as the only correct Catholic philosophical position (it was followed by the directives issued in the 1931 *Deus Scientarum Dominus* for the reorganization of ecclesiastical studies along strict Thomistic lines). The fourth condemned modernism, by which was meant the conciliation of Catholicism and modern science and particularly the acceptance of Newtonianism and Darwinism. An important step in the process of clarification and intellectual tightening was the dogma of papal infallibility in matters of faith and morals, approved by the twentieth ecumenical council (Vatican I) in 1870. The clarification strengthened the faithful, ridding them of doubts; it increased the appeal Catholicism has for educated people.

More important for times like the present was the revision of the Catholic position in mundane affairs. Until the end of the nineteenth century Catholicism sided with traditional political authoritarianism and—except for a few individuals, mostly French and Germans—had not faced social problems. Then came the change. In the Catholic nations of Europe non-Catholic forces had defeated traditional authoritarianism by the 1870's. Members of Catholic minorities in the United Kingdom and in the United States were the first to become aware of the protection democracy gave them. After 1870, non-Catholic (and often anti-Catholic) majorities or minorities were dominant in the Third French Republic, the Second German Empire, the Kingdom of Italy. In the late 1880's, for the first time, two high-ranking Church dignitaries—a French and an American cardinal—expressed approval of democracy. In 1890 the papacy cautiously authorized French Catholics to come to terms with the Republic. In Italy, partial authorization to participate in parliamentarian activities was given to Catholics before World War I; all restrictions were lifted when the war ended. The outcome of this political revision was the growth of Catholic parties, first in Europe, more recently in Latin America. In Italy, political Catholicism has reasserted itself. Defeated as an antiliberal force in 1859-70, it has become, as a democratic force, the dominant element in the Italian republic.

For most Europeans by the end of the nineteenth century social problems—the result of capitalistic industrialization—took precedence over all others. Pope Leo XIII and his advisers were aware of the need to outline a Catholic position in economic and social problems. The position received its first formulation in 1891 with the encyclical *Rerum Novarum*. It received further clarification with a number of other pronouncements, among which the most important have been the encyclicals *Quadragesimo Anno* of 1931 and *Mater ed Magistra* of 1963. The Catholic formula called corporatism—state-directed private enterprise functioning more through associative than competitive institutions—has found its place next to capitalism and collectivism. It has made possible, in Italy and elsewhere, a political alliance between Catholicism and democratic socialism. Because of Catholic discipline, the hold of the Church over the Italian Christian Democratic party is strong: Church principles are a guide to action and Church influence has so far been able to prevent divisions from degenerating into secessions.

The twenty-first Ecumenical Council, Vatican II, met in 1962 and continued in the following years. Held in Rome, it was not monopolized by Italian prelates, as the Council of Trent had been. It revealed the existence of significant divisions among the two or three thousand clerics forming the higher echelons of the clergy. It became evident that Catholic minorities in English-speaking and other nations had been deeply influenced by "errors" condemned in 1864. Again, not all Italian participants were on the side of tradition against innovation. Statements made by Pope John XXIII on points of doctrine and organization could be interpreted as expressing views defeated four centuries earlier in Trent. The line followed by Pope Paul VI, although more cautious than that of his predecessor, was a far cry from strict traditionalism. The future line of Roman Catholicism, in Italy and therefore in the world, is a question mark. Any change in Italy will affect the beliefs, thought, and politics of the millions who consider themselves Catholics.

FIVE

A Brilliant Era:

Twelfth to Fifteenth Centuries

Educated Italians consider the four centuries or so of the late Middle Ages and the Renaissance among the noblest in their history. Together with their national language, which took shape during that period, the Italians have inherited a legacy of treasured artistic masterpieces and literary classics which are an integral part of Italian culture today. But, taken as a whole, this period has left fewer traces in the way of life of the present Italian nation than those left by ancient Rome in legal institutions and political concepts, and by the early Middle Ages in religious beliefs and rituals. Little has survived of the concept of man, society, and life—of the ideas, values, and institutions—that fostered the creation of masterpieces and classics in the late Middle Ages and the Renaissance. The individual dynamism which gave these centuries their unique character came and went.

Any book on the background of the Italian nation is expected to mention twelfth and thirteenth century *comuni*, fourteenth century *signorie*, fifteenth century *principati*, artistic and literary revival, humanism, and the Renaissance. But the way of life that produced free and near-democratic commonwealths, absolute dictatorships, hereditary lordships, the creativity of freer minds; which was so turbulent that it was violent, and at the same time stimulated progress in all fields of endeavor, is alien to Italy today. Loss of independence and the re-establishment of religious discipline were the political and spiritual crises which ended the four brilliant centuries, transformed Italy, and gave birth to the modern Italian nation.

A New Life

Dynamism is an outstanding feature of the four-hundred or so years from the time when Gregory VII's *Dictatus* led to a violent clash between secular and ecclesiastical authoritarianism in the European community of Catholic nations, and the first years of the sixteenth century when a French king became ruler of the Milanese duchy in the north and a Spanish king added the Neapolitan state in the south to his possessions.

The four centuries are a fascinating period, when energy seemed to overflow in all directions. Individualism was the essential feature of national life. From it came dynamism and creativity, also lawlessness, turmoil, and much suffering. This was the time when the Italian nation, overrun for centuries by barbarians and deteriorated almost to their level, became for a while the mind and conscience of the expanding European Catholic world; when the Italian economy was the most advanced in Western Christendom, and middle class burghers of Italian cities lived better than powerful temporal and spiritual lords of other nations. Small Italian states then counted more than large transalpine kingdoms, and they chastised emperors and sultans on land and sea. Italian cities were the leading centers of intellectual life: Florence, Bologna, and Milan were for Western civilization then what New York, London, and Paris are today.

Twentieth century Italians find it hard to identify themselves with ancestors who lived and progressed in times of great, seemingly often unbearable, tension. There was the political tension related to factionalism within the independent communities, to rivalries between communities, to fear caused by repeated invasion and threats of invasion. There was, very often, also the inner tension of people trying to assert their own personalities, to discard preconceived and traditional ideas, and to free themselves from the control exercised formally or informally by the community. The inner tension helped to make for the greatness of the thinkers and artists. Dante the poet and Leonardo the scientist and painter were tormented men—as were thousands and thousands of other men of the period.

Twentieth century Italians do not recognize themselves in these humble ancestors who met in muddy town squares to organize their own governments, to elect their officials, to discuss their laws; in badly armed soldier-citizens who defied emperors and kings, were often defeated, and ended by asserting the independence of their city-states; in imaginative and venturesome business people who created new enterprises, transformed parts of Italy, and expanded the frontiers of Western commerce; in intellectuals who formulated new ideas and sometimes died for them.

This was the time when lived the most opprobrious criminals, for example the faction leaders and *signori* of the small cities of Romagna in the papal states, and some of the noblest saints of the Catholic Church—a mention of Francis of Assisi will suffice. It was a time when peace either of mind or among men seemed a foolish utopian dream, when a short phase of intense religiousness was followed by a long phase of unbelief and materialism. These were the centuries when the Italian nation produced original and powerful thinkers, from Arnold of Brescia and Thomas Aquinas to Marsilius of Padua and Machiavelli; when Italy produced the evangelical movements of the twelfth century and the humanism of the fifteenth; the astounding artistic flowering of the Renaissance; the factories in which worked hundreds of thousands of craftsmen and journeymen; the banking houses and commercial corporations of Florence, Genoa, Milan, and Venice, with branches not only everywhere in Catholic Europe but also in the Byzantine Near East and in the Arab Middle East; when Italy produced democratic republics and absolute dictatorships, and also the Venetian oligarchic constitution, admired for centuries by all who have longed for maximum political stability.

The synthesis of these four centuries is a difficult one. The common denominator is a larger measure of individual autonomy than before or after. It made for the environment in which grew Florentine republicanism in Tuscany and Viscontean despotism in Lombardy; which produced quiet mountain monasteries and the unrest of continual warfare; the absolute charity of early Franciscan monks and the absolute cruelty of Ezzelino da Romano; the intolerance of bigoted inquisitors and the tolerance of skeptical humanists. To this age belonged Lorenzo de' Medici, who treasured the good things of life, and Savonarola, who despised them; also Polo, who went east to China, and Columbus, who went west and failed to reach China. But a denominator is not a synthesis. The Italian scene of these four centuries is full of contrasts, varied and rich. It is life lived to the hilt.

At the end of the eleventh century and during the twelfth, the regions of northern and central Italy had witnessed the establishment of *comuni*, self-governing city states that at first were autonomous, later independent. Political liberty, vigorous for a couple of hundred years, gradually declined in the fourteenth and fifteenth centuries when government by the citizens was replaced with government by *signori*, lords whose temporary tenure soon became hereditary and whose power became increasingly absolute; today they would be called dictators. But liberty had lasted long enough to give the economy an impetus which carried it for centuries, well into the 1500's. In the Italian republican city-states factionalism, tension, and violence were only one side of the picture. Another side was the emancipation of economic activities. And the factionalism should not be exaggerated, considering that enough order prevailed to guarantee artisans and merchants the fruits of their labors and of their initiative.

From emancipation came an expansion of industrial and commercial activities which, already remarkable in the twelfth century, became more rapid during the next three hundred years. The expansion was the result of the hard work of hundreds of thousands of skilled craftsmen and of the imaginative initiative of businessmen. It did not spring naturally from an abundance of natural resources, which were no more plentiful in Italy than elsewhere in Europe; of capital, which was as scarce in Italy in the twelfth century as elsewhere (scarcer than in Moslem Spain); or of technological inventions. In the late Middle Ages Milan and Florence were financially what London was in the nineteenth century and New York is in the twentieth. The largest European merchant fleets were those of Pisa, Genoa, and Venice. Already at the end of the thirteenth century half a dozen Italian city-states counted for more economically than vast kingdoms beyond the Alps. Business families subsidized kings, pope, and emperor. Although unevenly, standards of living rose: populations of the Florentine, Milanese, and Venetian states were as prosperous in the fifteenth century as they were four hundred years later. The wealth produced was used in part to build magnificent palaces and town halls and countless churches and monasteries. It subsidized artists and writers. It also excited the greed of rulers of less advanced countries, and was a major factor in the invasions which led to the loss of Italian independence in the sixteenth century.

The Age of the Classics

Political and economic liberty are exceptions to the norm of authoritarian societies. As noble attempts to found the state on liberty rather than despotism, Italian *comuni* take their place next to ancient Mediterranean city-states and to contemporary North Atlantic democracies. A rarer exception to the norm of rigidly conforming societies has been intellectual liberty, the main source of change and progress. It is disliked by most, either because of arrogance or fear: the arrogance of those who claim to be depositories of the truth, the fear of those who dread new and disturbing ideas. Intellectual liberty is curbed more by the pressure of public opinion demanding conformity than by state-enforced or church-dictated censorship. A greater liberty of mind than before—or after, in the age of foreign dominations— was a salient feature of the last two centuries of this period and the source of the intellectual awakening and artistic flowering called the Renaissance.

Activities of the mind became freer more slowly than political and economic activities. For generations after the political emancipation of the *comuni*, it remained dangerous to think differently—as knew Arnold of Brescia, executed in the middle of the twelfth century; the evangelical preachers massacred by the Inquisition in the thirteenth century; and Francesco Stabili, executed early in the fourteenth century. But after the Great Interregnum annulled what remained of imperial authority in the second half of the thirteenth century—still more when Avignon's Babylonian Captivity annulled papal authority early in the fourteenth century—*comuni* and *signorie* of the no longer functioning kingdom of Italy and papal states became more lax in enforcing conformity.

Conditions arising from the long struggle between secular and ecclesiastical power emancipated many minds from dogmas, superstitions, and uncritically accepted commonplaces. As rulers of oligarchical and monarchical regional states were primarily concerned with power and wealth (and moreover often shared in the intellectual emancipation), they did not fully use the strength of the states they controlled to enforce intellectual conformity. From the first half of the fourteenth century until about two and a third centuries later, when the *rigoristi* faction led by Cardinal Caraffa (later Pope Paul IV) triumphed in Rome and organized the efficient modern Inquisition, people were suppressed in Italy for what they did, rarely for what they thought and said. Accusations of sorcery still brought savage punishment, but this was a special case. As a rule, political opposition was a crime, but intellectual deviation was not. Savonarola, burnt at the stake in Florence in 1498, had been condemned as a heretic but was executed for political deeds. Political reasons induced the irreligious Pope Alexander VI to authorize his trial. The Florentine Medici crowd rejoiced at Savonarola's death for political reasons; neither pope nor Medicis cared about the theological position of the Dominican monk. This indifference toward intellectual deviation explains the later attitude of Popes Leo X, Clement VII, and Paul III for so many years after Luther's statement of 1517: heresy did not bother them unduly until they became aware that it had political implications. Today, the separation of political despotism and control of the mind through state-enforced monopoly over communications media and education is inconceivable. However, it was possible in late fourteenth and in fifteenth century Italy.

As in many other instances in the history of mankind, the multiplicity of centers of political power helped to maintain a climate of relative freedom of expression. What Cangrande Della Scala and Guido Novello da Polenta had done for Dante Alighieri early in the fourteenth century, *signori* and princes did for countless writers and artists. The Venetian oligarchy was often willing to give shelter to those whose views led them into trouble in other Italian states. Fugitives from Florence were welcome in Siena, forty miles away. Gonzagas and Estes gave protection and subsidies to those whose life and liberty were threatened in the lands of the Sforzas and Medicis. *Signori* and princes gained prestige by surrounding themselves with distinguished writers and artists. Some freedom of expression was the price paid to attract writers and artists to the various courts.

What had been a desperately slow process of intellectual emancipation starting in the middle of the eleventh century acquired impetus three hundred years later. New ideas appeared, new values took root, new visions guided the artists. It was not much: the emancipation of minds was only partial and was limited to a numerically negligible section of the ten or twelve million Italians living at the time. But compared with what had been going on during the long, sad centuries of the European early Middle Ages, compared with what was going on elsewhere in most of Catholic Europe, intellectual emancipation was very advanced. There had been plenty of fore-runners, but the Italian Renaissance starts its brief life in the genera-tion that heaped scorn on the Bavarian Ludwig IV and the Luxem-burger Charles IV, that laughed at the hollow pretensions of em-perors without empire. More important, it was the generation that also laughed at the priests of a church whose heads were enjoying themselves in Avignon in the palace provided by princely cadets of the French kings.

Not many years had gone by since the time of the Hohenstaufen emperors, held in awe even when defeated on the battlefield; since the age of Pope Innocent III, who claimed that all Catholic rulers were his vassals; of St. Thomas, of the Inquisition, and of the sup-pression of evangelical believers. The laughter was the index of a revolution. This revolution was more important, in terms of the dif-ferent way of life which lasted until the middle of the sixteenth cen-tury, than political revolts and *coups d'état* in Sicily in 1282, in Venice in 1297, in Rome in 1347, in Florence in 1378. It was more important than the organizing of large banking enterprises and mer-chants' cooperative ventures in former city-states which had become the capitals of large regional states in the fourteenth century. Most Italians were shocked. Thoughtful people regretted, with Dante, the good old times. But the Renaissance, which had had its forerun-ners in the architects and chroniclers of the twelfth century, in the poets at the court of Frederick II in Palermo in the thirteenth cen-tury, in the Florentine writers who used Italian instead of Latin, in Cimabue's and Giotto's paintings, got under way with the genera-tion that read Boccaccio's *Decameron*. That generation allowed those willing to venture along new lines of thought to do so.

The freer use of the mind was the essence of the Renaissance. In the main areas into which Italy was divided politically, there was Ren-aissance in the measure that expression was free. The flowering took place in Florence but not in Palermo, where despotic Aragonese vice-roys had their headquarters. The Renaissance lasted as long as there was freedom of expression: in Venice longer than in other states because the Venetian government resisted the Spanish-backed Counter Reformation.

The freer way of life meant richness and variety of experience. It meant great achievements, in material and in spiritual fields. Among the many manifestations of the Renaissance was humanism, which was not mere erudition, but the application of critical thought to the astounding crop of ideas formulated by ancient thinkers. Humanists delighted in reading the works of Latin and Greek authors. They searched libraries for long-forgotten texts. From the time of Petrarch to that of Bembo, humanism was an essential feature of Italian life. It implied the priority of reasonableness over dogmatism; the tolerance described at the end of the seventeenth century in Great Britain as latitudinarianism; the concern for the individual frowned upon by all who postulate the priority of the group, whether a class, a congregation of believers, or the politically organized community. Italian humanism found disciples north of the Alps: in Germanic lands, in France, in England. It deeply influenced the spiritual and intellectual revolutions which occurred in those countries in the sixteenth century.

Tensions and dynamism made for a rich and lively literary scene. Neither before nor after this age did the Italian nation produce so many or such influential writers. Poets occupied the most distinguished place, and wrote about a wide range of subjects. Second, but very close, were historians, philosophers, and other prose writers. To the great output of original works should be added the translations from Latin and Greek, which considerably widened the intellectual horizon of Italians, and soon after of educated people in all nations of the European Catholic community.

Any list of authors in this age would seem discriminatory. So here we shall confine ourselves to the four who by general consent in Italy are not only the authors of classics (others share that distinction) but have been consistently read and are considered indispensable in the intellectual training of educated Italians. In chronological order they are: Dante, Petrarch, Boccaccio, and Machiavelli. It must be added that as influential as any of them is St. Thomas; however, his works are not for the general reader and their influence is therefore indirect.

The image Italians have of their four great classics may not be altogether accurate: what they actually say and what they are supposed to have said are not exactly the same thing. But the image still has a powerful effect. Thanks to Dante, a Tuscan dialect became the Italian language and as such had a unifying effect on a nation otherwise deeply divided. Dante's *Divine Comedy* is the most widely read and most heavily commented Italian literary classic. It contains much more than poetry: it is the statement of faith of a believer, a philosophical treatise, a great historical work, a forceful political tract. Freely mixing the Catholics' heavenly host with the Ancients' mythological figures, Dante completed the fusion of Christianity and paganism which had been the work of St. Gregory Magnus seven hundred years earlier. Dante familiarized Italians with the synthesis of scholasticism and Aristotelianism which had been the achievement of St. Thomas, and which has ever since been the philosophical foundation of Catholicism. By stressing the role of reason, Dante unwittingly prepared the ground for humanism. Thanks to him the decades on either side of 1300 are familiar to Italians; it is a period notable for the passage from small republican city-states in northern and central Italy to larger monarchical and oligarchic regional states. Dante's writings contributed powerfully to the cause of secularism versus clericalism. More important, they gave strong support to the cause of centralized government versus government by assemblies, i.e. of monarchism versus republicanism. Italian patriots of the nineteenth century, and nationalists of the twentieth, have seen in Dante a forerunner and have found his writings a source of inspiration.

Petrarch was one of the first humanists and the greatest of them all: he taught Italians admiration for the Ancients, and respect for the finer feelings. Petrarch's humanism was literary, but it was the foundation on which developed the dislike for violence and extremism that is characteristic of Italians, even if it is not a universal trait and if at times there have been active minorities bent on just these forms of action. Boccaccio told Italians that without being anti-Catholic one can, in Italy, be anticlerical, i.e. opposed to the paramount influence of the Catholic clergy. Ever since, except for the few generations curbed by the Counter Reformation, anticlericalism has been an important feature of Italian life, and it still is today. Machiavelli's work has been distorted in many ways. He left as his intellectual heritage three principles: politics are outside morality, might is right, the end justifies the means. According to the interpretation followed, Machiavellianism may or may not be attributed to Machiavelli; whatever the case, it has played its tragic role in Italian life for centuries, providing Italians with a justification for moral weakness.

Richness and variety of experience made for great tension and considerable suffering. Violence, cruelty, conflicts of all kinds made the history of Renaissance Italy a tragic one, as much so for the passive masses as for the active participants in the events of the times. Unlike Christianity a thousand years earlier, unlike socialism in the twentieth century, the Renaissance ushered in a way of life that, though it was dynamic and turbulent, characterized a minority only. With few exceptions—the most notable being urban Florentines and Romans—the Italian masses continued to live their traditional life founded on conformity and obedience to authority. They sighed with relief when, in the sixteenth century, the despotism of foreign rulers and of native clericalism curbed minds and consciences, so putting an end to the exhausting effervescence of the educated minority.

SIX

FOREIGN DOMINATIONS

IN MODERN TIMES

The great literary and other artistic works of the communal and Renaissance period of Italian history remained for posterity. But the spirit in which they were created disappeared. The religious and intellectual crisis of the middle of the sixteenth century obliterated ideas, values, and attitudes which had been influential during the previous centuries. The outcome of the crisis was largely determined by the pressure exercised by Spain, which early in the sixteenth century already ruled half of Italy, and soon after was to exercise paramount power over most of the rest.

Italian historians call the post-Renaissance period the era of foreign dominations, although at no time was the Italian nation totally subjected to foreign rule. Spanish, Austrian (German), and French dominations are still present in memories that have stayed alive through the generations, in traits common to many Italians, in aspects of everyday life. The Spaniards deeply influenced the south, the French and Germans parts of the north. This is the period when the nation acquired characteristics by which it is still known today, and which slow down the process of change. Italy having become a backwater in the stream of European life during this period, standard textbooks often cover it with a few lines. But because of their role in shaping the Italian nation of today, the student of Italy cannot ignore the foreign dominations.

The End of Independence

Foreign powers ruled or exercised a dominant influence on Italy for twelve generations, from around 1500 until 1859-60. It all began with requests, made first by the duke of Milan and a few years later by the government of the Venetian republic, to Charles VIII of France and his successor Louis XII to help them expand at the expense of other Italian states. Writing a few decades later, the Florentine historian and statesman Guicciardini described Italy in the early 1490's as being at peace, independent, prosperous, densely populated, rich in splendid cities and distinguished men, governed by wise statesmen and magnificent and generous princes. There was some exaggeration in this description, but also much that was true. In 1500 Italy was to Catholic Europe what, in 1914, Europe was to the rest of the world: small in size but politically influential, in the lead culturally and economically. In thirty years, 1500-1530, the influence and leadership disappeared—just as four centuries later, in thirty-one years 1914-1945, European influence and leadership vanished.

In 1500 the Italian "great powers" consisted of five states. In the south, the kingdom of Naples accounted for nearly one-fourth of the area of Italy, and for about one-fifth of the ten to twelve million inhabitants the country had at the time. In Naples reigned Frederic III, cousin of Ferdinand II, the king of Aragon who united Spain through his marriage to Isabella of Castile and his conquest of Moslem Granada in 1492 and Navarre in 1512. King Frederic had little authority: feudalism had come late to southern Italy, with the Normans; it was still strong there when it no longer existed, as a political system, in the rest of Italy. The kingdom of Naples was living largely on its past reputation. Weak (as it really was) and reputedly rich (which it was no longer), it was a natural goal for ambitious foreign princes.

Half its size and with two-thirds its population, but considerably wealthier than Naples (actually the richest European state of all), was the northeastern republic of Venice, known as the *Serenissima*. Its area was doubled by well-administered dependencies in the western Balkans and the eastern Mediterranean. Commerce, industry, and agriculture flourished in the Venetian state, which was strong enough to hold its own against the pressure of the fast-expanding Ottoman empire. In Venice ruled a small closed oligarchy of wealthy, highly educated, competent business people, equally conversant with economic and political affairs, patrons of art and letters. Their position was consolidated through a *coup d'état* in 1297; they governed the republic until 1797, most of the time with remarkable efficiency. No country in Europe has ever enjoyed five hundred years of political stability, as the Venetian republic did.

The duchy of Milan, in the North, covered an area about one-third the size of the kingdom of Naples, with over a million inhabitants and a large revenue, the result not of fiscal exploitation but of economic prosperity. Beginning in 1479 the duchy was governed by Lodovico Sforza (first as regent for his young nephew, then as duke after the nephew's death, attributed by contemporaries to poison). Sforza was intelligent, ruthless, ambitious, also a munificent patron of the arts.

The republic of Florence in central Italy had half the area and population of the duchy of Milan, but almost as much wealth. Industry and banking had made it prosperous. Since the thirteenth century it had produced more distinguished men than any other part of Italy. A revolt late in 1494 expelled the Medici family, which had achieved power in 1434 when Cosimo the Elder was head of the popular or democratic party, and had ruled the state despotically under Cosimo and his grandson Lorenzo the Magnificent. Governed in 1500 by a large open oligarchy, the citizens of the Florentine republic enjoyed greater liberty than other Italians.

The papal states, fifth of the major powers, were large on the map. However, not counting Rome, only small districts were governed by the papal administration. The rest were ruled by local despots, nominally as papal vicars, in reality as independent monarchs. Bloody feuding was a feature of their rule. The pope at this time was Alexander VI, Rodrigo Borgia, whose son Caesar was made duke of Romagna and was intent, from 1500-1503, through murders and treachery, on making his rule effective. The large papal income was obtained only in small part from taxation in the papal states; most came from gifts, offerings, tributes, and tithes from all over Catholic Europe, from the sale of indulgences, and from a brisk trade in holy relics (mostly fakes).

Not counting several minuscule principalities and republics, there were in Italy, besides the five major states, a score of smaller ones.

Those in a position to play a political role were Ferrara, whose dukes acquired a fortune by manufacturing cannons, and the oligarchic republic of Genoa, whose wealthy citizens owned many ships and controlled vast financial interests. North of Genoa was the duchy of Savoy, which included most of Piedmont; it was larger than Milan, but underpopulated and poor, more French than Italian. The island kingdoms of Sicily and Sardinia had kept their institutions, but were not independent. Sicily, through dynastic succession in 1409, and Sardinia through occupation in the fourteenth century, had come under the rule of the kings of Aragon, later kings of Spain.

Such was Italy in 1500. Some of the European transalpine states had experienced developments amounting to revolutionary changes. In 1492 the centuries-old conflict between Catholics and Moslems in Spain ended. Culturally inferior to the Moslems, the Catholics were victorious largely because of the efficient military organization in the kingdom of Castile. Here there was now a strong and well-armed state. The Spanish king and queen, Ferdinand II of Aragon and Isabella of Castile, were as yet little interested in the far lands on which in 1492 their Genoese admiral Christopher Columbus had planted the Christian cross and the Castilian flag. The defeat of the Moslems opened the road to other conquests. Sicily and Sardinia were already governed by Spanish viceroys; Naples had been briefly united to Aragon at the middle of the fifteenth century and was now ruled by an illegitimate branch of the house of Aragon. The Neapolitan public revenue—twice as large as Spain's—was tempting to an ambitious and unscrupulous ruler.

In France, the able Louis XI had successfully reorganized the state, which had been weakened by civil and foreign wars lasting for generations. Here again, at the end of the fifteenth century, were the elements that make for imperialism: centralized authority, a strong military establishment, a sound treasury. Bureaucratic efficiency was giving the French nation the cohesion that religious zeal had given to Catholic Spaniards. Then, dynastic claims held the place of today's geographical, historical, and ethnic claims in countries strong enough to attack their neighbors. At the pope's request a French royal prince, Charles of Anjou, had in 1266 conquered the Two Sicilies. His last direct descendant, Queen Joan, had named as heir (among others) a

French cousin whose claims reverted to the royal main branch of the family. So Louis XI's son, Charles VIII, found plenty of justification for an attack on Naples. Louis XII, cousin and successor of Charles VIII, had equally valid dynastic claims on the duchy of Milan, through an ancestress who was the daughter of a Milanese duke.

Germanic Europe was politically fragmented, but the archduke of Austria, Maximillian of Hapsburg, chosen emperor by the seven electors in 1493, was trying to make good his claims as effective ruler of the ancestral domains in Germany. He coveted the financial resources of the wealthy Italian states, which he needed to strengthen his position in Germany. Swiss cantons looked hungrily at the Italian valleys on the south side of the Alps.

Fearful of being attacked by a coalition of Venice, Florence, and Naples, Ludovico Sforza of Milan promised his support to Charles VIII of France should he decide to carry through his claims on Naples. The French king came in 1494. He attacked Florence, entered Rome peacefully, and occupied Naples early in 1495 without fighting, the Neapolitan king having been abandoned by his feudatories. Sickness among the troops, and the formation of a European anti-French coalition, speeded Charles's return to France. Except for the change of government in Florence everything went back to normal in Italy, but the French raid demonstrated that Italian states either had no military strength or they were unwilling to use what they had.

In 1499 the Venetian government promised to support Louis XII, successor of Charles, if he should come to claim Milan. The duchy was to be partitioned between the French king and Venice. Louis XII failed in 1499 but succeeded in 1500, and the French remained in possession of the duchy of Milan for most of the first quarter of the century. Not satisfied with Milan, at the end of 1500 Louis XII, at the instigation of Pope Alexander VI, signed a treaty with his Spanish colleague for the partition of the kingdom of Naples. The northern half was for the French, the southern for the Spaniards. Late in 1501 the French conquest was completed, with little fighting. Dividing the spoils created the usual problem of exactly what should go to whom. The disputed area was around Foggia. Then, in 1502, the Spaniards fought the French, the first in a series of wars lasting until 1559. Spanish infantry proved more efficient than French cavalry.

Defeated in 1503, the French withdrew. The kingdom of Naples joined Sicily and Sardinia as Spanish viceroyalties. Two-fifths of Italy was in the hands of either the Spaniards or the French.

In 1508 came still another round of wars. This time Venice was to be deprived of most of her possessions by the kings of France and Spain, Emperor Maximilian, and Pope Julius II Della Rovere. The main attack was made by the French. The Venetians were defeated but did not surrender. Fearful of the French, their allies made a coalition which was joined by the king of England. A French defeat enabled Venice to recover most of her territories. The Spaniards kept the Apulian cities which had been under Venetian rule, and in 1512 re-established the Medicis in Florence and the Sforzas in Milan. Young Francis I of France, cousin and successor of Louis XII, made an alliance with Venice and in 1515 defeated the coalition formed by Ferdinand II of Spain, his two puppets in Florence and Milan, Emperor Maximilian, the Swiss Confederation, and Pope Leo X (a Florentine Medici). This was the last international war to be fought by the Swiss Confederation. After their victory the French went back to Milan.

Next there came a short lull, largely because the French were satisfied with their success, and because the death of Ferdinand of Spain was followed by that of Emperor Maximilian. Both were succeeded by their grandson, the able Flemish-speaking youth Charles V. A revolt against monarchical despotism (the last until 1820) was quashed in Spain in 1521. After that, Charles V took over where his two grandfathers had left off in 1515. In 1525 Francis I was soundly beaten at Pavia, near Milan, and captured. Once again, a Sforza returned to Milan under Spanish protection. His independence was purely nominal. In 1535 the Spaniards took over the administration of the duchy of Milan, which in 1556 became an appanage of the Spanish crown. Pope Clement VII (another Medici) having intrigued with France, in 1527 Charles V sent an army against Rome. According to contemporaries, the sack of Rome was on a level with the devastations of Visigoths and Vandals in the fifth century. The population fell to an all-time low, under twenty thousand. In 1528 Admiral Doria, the Genoese commander of Charles V's naval forces, captured his native city and ruled it as a Spanish puppet. Coming to terms with Charles V, Pope Clement VII crowned him emperor and king of Italy early in 1530, in Bologna. In exchange, the pope asked for the re-establishment of his family's rule in Florence, from which the Medicis had been expelled a second time in 1527. The Spanish imperial army attacked the Florentine republic and besieged Florence; the treachery of a mercenary commanding Florentine troops ended the war early in August 1530. A Medici was made duke by Charles V. A chapter of Italian history that had begun in the eleventh century came to an end.

Usually it takes time to consolidate a new rule, native or foreign. Not everyone is willing to give up old loyalties and old ideals. There was gradually declining unrest in Italy until 1559, partly linked to the wars still being waged by Francis I of France and his son, Henry II, against Charles V and his son, Philip II. In 1536 the French occupied the duchy of Savoy-Piedmont and held it for twenty-three years, until a Spanish victory enabled the young duke Emmanuel Philibert to recover his ancestral domains. (He did not however regain districts north and east of the lake of Geneva, annexed by Swiss cantons.) The Spanish puppet ruling in Mantua annexed the duchy of Montferrat, in northwestern Italy. The pope was helped by the Spaniards to establish his direct rule over the duchy of Camerino.

In 1554 the duke of Florence, with Spanish aid, attacked the republic of Siena, which was friendly to the French. The city was captured in 1555, and about two hundred families withdrew to the hill town of Montalcino, where they defended themselves until 1559. The duke of Florence later received from the pope the title of grand duke of Tuscany. Sienese coastal districts were annexed by Spain in 1557, and formed the Stato dei Presidî. There were conspiracies in Florence, Genoa, Lucca, Piacenza. Those that aimed at re-establishing independence or republican liberties, or both, failed. There were revolts or *coups d'état* in Corsica (a Genoese possession), Perugia, Siena, and other cities. They failed. The establishment of the Inquisition led to rioting in Naples and Rome, but it was quickly suppressed. By 1559, when the French and Spaniards signed the peace of Cateau-Cambrésis, all was over in Italy. With their viceroys and governors in Naples, Sicily, Sardinia, Milan, and the Stato dei Presidî, Spain ruled directly over two-fifths of Italy. The rulers of most other Italian states were Spanish puppets. Only the republic of Venice remained independent not only in name but in fact, though it was sandwiched between the Italian possessions of the Spanish Hapsburgs and the Alpine possessions of the Austrian Hapsburgs and was hard pressed by Ottoman Turks in the Balkans and the Mediterranean.

Spanish Hegemony

The Spanish domination, established in 1503-1530 and consolidated in 1530-1559, lasted until the beginning of the eighteenth century. According to one's point of view, Spanish hegemony did good or harm to the Italian nation. In those centuries, Spain was more than a nation and a state, it was a way of life. Admirable in many respects (piety and scorn for material things, discipline, loyalty, dependability, moral integrity), this way of life negated what was making for progress in other nations: liberty understood as man's right and duty to act according to his own rationally reached decisions, conscious use of rational faculties, a dose of materialism.

In the two generations following the final defeat of Moslem Spaniards, Catholic Spain conquered a vast European and transoceanic empire. The conquest primarily resulted from the fact that Spain had the military efficiency and centralization of power to serve her political ambitions, religious zeal, and greed. While conquering, Spain declined economically. A nation honoring religious vocation and military discipline can hardly provide a favorable environment for the growth of business activities; the remarkable medieval prosperity of the Iberian peninsula had been chiefly the work of Moslems and Jews, who did not long survive the Catholic triumph—not even when they tried to save themselves through conversion. By the beginning of the seventeenth century the non-Catholic minorities (a quarter of the total Spanish population) had been liquidated. With them disappeared their industrial and commercial enterprises, their agricultural efficiency, their intellectual curiosity.

What happened in Spain happened in Spanish possessions as well. The Neapolitan kingdom and Sicily were declining before Ferdinand's viceroys began to govern, and the decline continued. The duchy of Milan was wealthy in 1500. The devastations caused by the many wars fought there between French and Spaniards led to a decline which continued under Spanish rule. Italian puppet states followed the Spanish trend. Economic vigor died along with intellectual vigor. An index of the general stagnation is that the population of Italy in

1700 was about the same as in 1500. Italians settled into a quiet, un-
eventful, unexciting life. For most it was a peaceful life, agreeable
even if obtained by acceptance of poverty, servility, and ignorance.

It is difficult to say which of the two main developments of the
sixteenth century in Italy—the Counter Reformation or the establishment of Spanish domination—had the greater influence in molding
the contemporary Italian nation. The two developments helped each
other. They combined to produce conformity, deviousness, and docility; to create the conviction that governmental authority is beyond
the reach of common people, that the hierarchical order is the natural
order. Whatever their respective influence, the outcome was a radical
transformation in national character, as radical as the transformation
of Roman Italians in the fourth and fifth centuries.

Partial exceptions to the general trend were the two northern
border states of Venice and Savoy-Piedmont. There was decline in
the Venetian republic too, but it was slower and started later than in
the Spanish-dominated areas. Venice was the last refuge of the artistic
and literary Renaissance; as late as the early seventeenth century there
was some freedom of expression in the *Serenissima*. But the wars
against the Ottoman empire were a constant drain. In spite of the
naval victory of Lepanto in 1571, won by a coalition of Catholic states,
the Venetians were compelled to abandon Cyprus two years later.
Another century went by and after long and fierce fighting the Turks
conquered Crete. It was a sign of Venetian political decline that in
the seventeenth century the ambassadors of the smaller and less populous, but wealthier and stronger, Dutch republic took diplomatic
precedence over the ambassadors of the *Serenissima*. Like most of
continental Europe Venice was frightened by the Turkish siege of
Vienna in 1683, and so joined the Holy League formed in 1684 by
Austria and Poland, which Russia too joined later. The League waged
war successfully against the Ottoman empire, liberating Hungary and
Transylvania in central Europe, Azov in southern Russia, and Morea
in the Balkans. For Venice, however, it was a short-lived success, annulled by defeats and losses suffered in the next war of 1714-1718.

In the duchy of Savoy-Piedmont at the end of the sixteenth century
was created, on a militia basis, the strong military organization which
was—with varying degrees of efficiency—the main feature of the
state until it merged into the kingdom of Italy in 1861. Duke Em-

manuel Philibert, in particular, did for Savoy-Piedmont what the Hohenzollern Great Elector Frederick William was to do for Prussia-Brandenburg a hundred years later. On their military strength was founded the role the two states played in the nineteenth century in the unification of Italy and Germany respectively. Between 1536 and 1601 the Savoy dukes lost nearly half of their transalpine territories, but between 1601 and 1748 they extended their possessions in northern Italy considerably, through the annexation first of Saluzzo, later of Montferrat and other smaller states and through encroachments on Milan. When the war of Spanish succession ended, the Italian component of the state (Piedmont) prevailed over the French (Savoy). After having held Sicily for five years (1713-1718), Victor Amadeus II of Savoy-Piedmont exchanged it in 1720 for Sardinia, which—together with the royal title—gave the state its name.

Austrian Hegemony

Spanish domination was followed by about a century and a half of direct Austrian rule in parts of Italy and hegemony over most of the rest. An eighteen-year French interlude (1796-1814) divides the era of Austrian domination into two periods, unequal in length and profoundly different in character. The first period goes from 1706 (occupation of Milan by Austrian troops) and 1707 (occupation of Naples) to the defeats inflicted on the Austrians by the French revotionary troops in the spectacular campaign of 1796 led by the young Corsican general Napoleon Bonaparte. During this period, Austrian influence played—rather paradoxically—a progressive role, in that it had an emancipating effect and promoted a partial awakening of the Italian educated classes. The second period goes from 1814 to 1859. This time Austrian influence played a completely reactionary role, acting as a brake to changes advocated by the liberal and patriotic minority in the nation. The brake functioned through the usual means: police repression and terrorism made possible by superior military strength, and censorship made possible because the ecclesiastical organization, working with the Austrian authorities, held a monopoly over education and communications media.

Except for the name, the capital, and memories, there is nothing in common between the present Austrian republic and the Austrian multinational state of the eighteenth and nineteenth centuries, which so deeply influenced Italian developments. When Charles V abdi-cated, the Hapsburg possessions in south Germany (Austria and other districts) went to his brother Ferdinand, already king of Bo-hemia and of the part of Hungary not ruled by Ottoman Turks. This Austrian state acquired cohesion and distinctiveness when Ferdinand's successors used identical repressive measures to enforce the Counter Reformation in all their dominions, and to re-establish the undisputed sway of Catholicism. Protestantism was eradicated, Czechs became subjects, Hungarian autonomy was curtailed. By 1700, when an Austrian Hapsburg claimed the succession in Spain against a French Bourbon, the Austrian state was the largest in Catholic Europe, and inferior in population only to France. It was the dominant power in Germany. It had a large enough revenue to maintain a strong military establishment and to buy the services of able generals.

The treaties of Utrecht and Rastadt, which ended the war of Span-ish succession in 1713-14, recognized the French Bourbon pretender, Philip V, as king of Spain. They also transferred to the Austrian Hapsburg, Charles VI, all Spanish possessions in the Lowlands and Italy, except for the island of Sicily (which went to Amadeus II of Savoy-Piedmont). To these possessions was added the duchy of Man-tua. In 1718 a successful Spanish raid briefly re-established Spanish rule in Sicily. A European coalition compelled Spain to surrender Sicily to Austria, which compensated Victor Amadeus with Sardinia. In another war, caused by conflicting monarchist interests in relation to the Polish throne, Austrian troops were defeated in Italy by the French and their allies. Neapolitans and Sicilians hailed the Spaniards as liberators—a clear indication that two centuries of Spanish rule had created a strong sense of loyalty to Spain. At the peace treaty of Vienna in 1738, the kingdoms of Naples and Sicily were trans-ferred to a younger son of the king of Spain, on condition that the two Italian states would never be reunited to Spain.

Charles III of Naples and Sicily, although a Spanish Bourbon, was more French than Spanish. He had been educated in an environment where French cultural and political influences were strong; he looked to the king of France as head of the family and counted on his pro-tection in case of danger. Also, Charles chose as his ministers Italians who had been deeply influenced by French progressive ideas. In 1737 Austrian control was established in Tuscany. Through agreements

among the major European powers, the successor to the last Medici
was Francis of Lorraine, son-in-law of the Hapsburg Charles VI, and
later emperor and co-ruler of Austria with his wife Maria Teresa.
Origin and education made Francis more French than German. As
the result of dynastic arrangements, a small duchy in northern Italy
went to a brother of Charles III of Naples and another, a little later,
to a younger son of Francis and Maria Teresa. When in 1748 the peace
of Aix-la-Chapelle ended the third major war of succession fought by
Europeans in that century (the war of the Austrian succession), Austria ruled in Italy a reduced Milanese duchy and Tuscany. Even if
Austrian political influence was strong everywhere—thanks to military superiority—Austrian hegemony in Italy was less absolute than
Spanish hegemony had been. Moreover (and particularly in the two
areas ruled by Austria), there was sufficient loosening of censorship to
provide some scope for the stimulus of relatively free discussion, and
to enable foreign ideas to reach educated people.

In an authoritarian, hierarchical society like that of Italy in the
middle of the eighteenth century, change usually comes from above.
Only those who belong, or are close, to the ruling class can risk de-
parting from accepted ways and have the power to do so. While the
masses remained supine, some of the princes, foreign governors, and
their ministers tried to alter existing institutions. They aimed at
strengthening their rule, at making political absolutism more absolute,
with faith in the commonplace that these steps are short cuts to
government efficiency. They ended, paradoxically, by weakening the
authoritarian structure. Liberal ideas of French and British origin
began to circulate, to provide the foundation for aspirations of Italian
revolutionary patriots in the nineteenth century. Groups that were
forerunners of the secret societies agitating later for independence,
unification, constitutionalism, and democracy were organized.

The Bourbon and Hapsburg-Lorraine princes ruling Italian states
that included nearly half the area of the country and more than half
its population frankly aimed at strengthening absolutism. To achieve
this aim, and on the advice of ministers who had assimilated ideas
put forth by French *philosophes* concerned with progress, they introduced policies to weaken the privileged classes (aristocracy and clergy)
and increase the number of efficient active citizens who would make

competent officials, good soldiers, industrious and productive artisans and farmers. The weakening of the priviliged classes—bulwark of traditionalism—meant the suppression of the last residues of feudal rights and thus the emancipation of the rural masses; the equalization of laws and particularly the end of separate ecclesiastical jurisdiction; and greater religious tolerance and less severe censorship (newspapers and magazines began to appear in the 1760's). The number of efficient and active citizens was increased by setting up new schools and partially secularizing education, and through the application of economic reforms advocated by the French *physiocrates* and later by Adam Smith. All this amounted to a revolution.

The example set by Hapsburg-Lorraine and Bourbon princes was imitated to some extent by Charles Emmanuel III of Savoy, king of Sardinia from 1730 to 1773. Within the Venetian and Genoese business oligarchies, a few people began to think in terms of reforms, but nothing was actually done. There was no change in the papal states either, except that in 1773 Pope Clement XIV was compelled, by a coalition of Catholic rulers bent on increasing state power at the expense of the Church's, to dissolve the Jesuit order which since its formation in the 1530's had been the main pillar of the papacy. When the revolution broke out in France in 1789, Italian states governed by native authorities had the negative distinction of being more traditionalist and reactionary than those which, through European wars and dynastic arrangements, had come under the rule of foreign sovereigns.

The exit of Spanish officials and garrisons from the Italian scene had weakened the heavy crust of authoritarian institutions which had repressed the creativity so evident during the dynamic and turbulent communal and Renaissance era. Writers and scientists like Tasso, Bruno, and Boccalini had known, late in the sixteenth and early in the seventeenth centuries, the meaning of the pressure of an absolute state, serving an absolute Church or being served by it. Now the pressure lifted, but it took more than a generation after the end of the war of Spanish succession for results to appear, linked to new conditions and a new situation. At the middle of the eighteenth century there was evidence of a new life, at least in some classes of the population in some parts of Italy. Great progressive thinkers like Sarpi,

Campanella, and Galileo early in the seventeenth century, and Vico, Muratori, and Giannone (who died in prison) a hundred years later, were isolated individuals, with little or no influence over their contemporaries. After 1750, antitraditional progressive attitudes and thinking were sufficiently diffused to set a new tone among educated people.

Milan and Naples, in the second half of the eighteenth century, were the two cities where one could meet the largest groups of liberal-minded Italians. In Milan lived Beccaria, the best-known Italian *philosophe* of that generation, the brothers Verri, the poet Parini, the naturalist Spallanzani, and the physicists Galvani and Volta. In Naples lived Genovesi, the first European to occupy a university chair in economics (1754), Galiani, another economist, the jurist Filangieri, the political scientist Pagano. In a few cities liberal-minded Italians were able to join associations and clubs, the first step toward political action. Influential in the 1760's were the Milanese *Circolo dei Pugni* and the Florentine *Georgofili*. But even in Milan and Tuscany the authorities kept a careful eye on political and intellectual dissidents, and elsewhere any kind of association was strictly forbidden. To escape police and censors, those who shared progressive ideas (the moderate but implicitly revolutionary ideas of Voltaire and Montesquieu, of Locke and Adam Smith) met in the secret lodges of the clandestine freemasonry, the most important—but by no means the only—organization to give cohesion to the continental liberal movement in the eighteenth century. Standing for religious tolerance, greater freedom of the press, wider constitutionalism, and against restrictive and protectionist mercantilism, the freemasons had originated in Great Britain, acquired a foothold in France before 1720, and from there had spread to most nations of Europe. In Italy they were the bearers of the ideas of the French Enlightenment. Their political and intellectual influence continued through the nineteenth century and did not wane until the twentieth. Political absolutism and clericalism were their enemies—the absolute state and the absolute church. Also from France came Jansenism, which spread among Italian Catholics in the eighteenth century; in its opposition to the centralized authority of the pope and in its basic equalitarianism, it acted as a liberal, antitraditionalist force. Centers of Jansenism included Tuscany, the university of Pavia near Milan, Parma, and Genoa.

French Hegemony

This period of Austrian influence ended in 1796. Since the autumn of 1792 the newly established French republic had been at war with its Italian neighbor, the kingdom of Sardinia. The French-speaking districts of Savoy and Nice had been overrun and annexed by France, but war had been at a standstill for three years along the Alpine ranges when twenty-seven-year-old Napoleon Bonaparte was given the command of the French troops. In a few weeks he reorganized the 36,000 badly equipped men. In April 1796 he won his first victories against Sardinians and Austrians. In May he entered Milan. Republican states—France's satellites—were organized in northern Italy. Bonaparte returned to Paris at the end of 1797, but the French advance continued. Rome was occupied in 1798, and a Roman republic proclaimed. Then came the turn of Tuscany, of Piedmont, and, early in 1799, of Naples. The French suffered reverses in Italy while Bonaparte was in Egypt; his return and victory at Marengo in 1800 reestablished French control. The Austrians had been given Venice in 1797 and they kept it until 1806. Tuscany was annexed to France in 1808, Rome the following year. Political boundaries changed incessantly. A small Cispadane republic was formed late in 1796, expanded to become a Cisalpine, then an Italian, republic; finally it became an Italian kingdom including about a third of the country, of which Bonaparte made himself king in 1805. Its government was entrusted to his loyal and capable stepson, Eugène de Beauharnais. Nearly a third of Italy was annexed to France: Piedmont, Liguria, Tuscany, Latium, and other districts. Bonaparte first made a brother king of Naples, then his brother-in-law Murat. In 1809 only the islands of Sicily and Sardinia, protected by the British navy, remained outside French control. For several years Sicily was actually governed by the British who tried, with little success, to liberalize the institutions of the island.

French domination was a tornado. It lasted only a short time but it had enormous impact. It swept away an old structure. It destroyed the institutions that held in rigid bonds what had become the traditional Italian way of life inherited from the Counter Reformation and the Spanish domination. When the tornado blew over the institutions

were re-established, but they were not as solid as before. The values
supporting them had become more vulnerable. The Italian populace
remained consistently hostile to the French, who had, on the contrary,
been received with enthusiasm by the small minority of educated
Italians fired by the ideas, values, and aspirations of the French Enlightenment and the French Revolution.

In "Liberty, Equality, Fraternity" were included ideas such as progress, national sovereignty, popular government, freedom of conscience
and of the press, social justice, the end of privilege and of restrictive
economic practices, legal and moral equality, education for all, scientific inquiry, materialism. These ideas were the negation of everything
implicit in Italian authoritarian, hierarchical, stagnant traditionalism.
The process of awakening, which had begun on a small scale in the
generation reaching maturity around the middle of the eighteenth
century, gained impetus under the stimulus of the French Revolution at the end of the century. It became the patriotic, liberal, and
democratic *Risorgimento* (Resurgence) of the nineteenth century
and, with ups and downs, has expanded to include ever wider sections
of the nation. A manifestation of this same process was the Resistance
movement against fascism and its German ally in the twentieth century. The awakening is now reaching the hitherto untouched sectors
of the nation. In the measure in which it expands, a new nation re-
places that formed during the spiritual and political crises of the sixteenth century.

The small liberal minority of the 1790's, formed chiefly of the progressive part of the upper classes, took advantage of the presence of
French revolutionary armies to organize short-lived democratic republics. When it became clear, in 1802-1805, that the French had come
to Italy not to liberate but to stay, there was a split among liberal-
minded progressive Italians. Most continued to give their loyal support to French rule, which they considered an improvement over the
ancien régime and which introduced administrative, judicial, ecclesiastical, educational, and economic reforms on a bigger scale than had
been achieved by the reforming princes of the eighteenth century. A
few remained aloof, or became clandestine opponents, making it clear
that their opposition to despotism and foreign rule did not exclude
the French. Around 1807 or 1808, members of the latter group began
to organize—at first as a radical offshoot of the pro-French freema-

sonry—the clandestine movement of the *carbonari* (charcoal burners), which played a revolutionary role in the 1820's and early 1830's.

In the winter of 1813-14, Bonaparte's vast European empire collapsed under the blows of an anti-French coalition led by Great Britain, Russia, and Austria. Habits of docility in Italy were a result of nearly three hundred years of foreign domination. So there was no general insurrection against the French in Italy, as there had been instead in Spain since 1808 and as there was in Germany in 1813. Neither was there any opposition to the large Austrian forces and the smaller British ones which occupied the country. Two attempts were made in 1814-15 to spare Italy further foreign domination, and both failed. The first aimed at saving the existing kingdom of Italy. In April 1814 a provisional government was organized in Milan; it hoped for British support, but the British government decided to leave a free hand to the Austrians, who occupied Milan in May. The second attempt, supported by both freemasons and *carbonari*, aimed at creating a united constitutional state under the king of Naples, Murat, who had deserted Bonaparte in the hour of crisis. Murat counted on the loyalty of the Neapolitan army and the support of the Italian nation. He had neither. In May 1815 Austrian troops were in control of the kingdom of Naples. Murat fled. He returned a few months later with a small band of veterans and exiles, was captured and executed. Ironically, a Frenchman was the first to die in the nineteenth century attempts to unify Italy.

ITALY IN 1859

SEVEN

LIBERAL ASCENDANCY

IN THE NINETEENTH CENTURY

Between the re-establishment of Austrian hegemony in 1814-15 and the Fascist seizure of power in 1922, the term "liberal" was applied to three different groups in Italy. At first, briefly, it denoted all enemies of traditionalism, the revolutionaries opposed to despotism. Later the term was applied only to the moderates among the revolutionaries, those who advocated a united parliamentarian state. Early in the twentieth century (and spelled with a capital "L") it indicated the group formed by the amalgamation of the parliamentarian right and left of the previous generation, now united against growing extremist forces.

In its various connotations, liberalism played an important role in Italian life. As a general movement, it agitated against foreign domination, absolutism, and clericalism. As a moderate tendency, it kept the upper hand during the revolutionary 1859-60 period. The 1861-1922 state is known in Italy as the "Liberal" state. Liberals were always a minority, not even a large one. Their numbers increased for several decades, then declined, at least relatively to the size of the population. Foreign support helped them to unify Italy. After unification, they were kept in power until 1922 by limited suffrage, the multiplicity of their opponents, and the apathy of the masses.

The unification of Italy in 1859-70 was the major achievement in this period. It ended a political fragmentation that had lasted thirteen centuries. Another major development was the gradual transformation of Catholicism: in the long run this may prove to be the more important event. A major change was that Italians were shaking off their economic torpor and standards of living began to improve. Intellectually this era comes second only to the Renaissance. Even before unification there was in one Italian state or another sufficient freedom to enable artists and writers to express themselves. Freedom became general after the unification. Tension, caused by the contrast between aspirations and reality, raised the level of creativity. There were great composers, great poets, the novelist Manzoni, thinkers among whom the most influential were Mazzini and Croce.

This was the period during which were formed the major political divisions in the Italian nation today. The pre-unification traditionalists correspond to the right of the Christian Democratic party. From them, at the end of the nineteenth century, seceded the advocates of a Catholic democratic movement, who founded the Popular party in 1919 and are now the dominant element in the Christian Democratic party. The traditionalists' original opponents are today's Liberals and Republicans. Socialism became organized in the 1890's, and already clear in the first decade of the twentieth century were the tendencies that led to the Social Democratic, Socialist, Unitarian Socialist, and Communist parties of the 1960's. Patriots disappointed in their expectations of national greatness gathered in the Nationalist party before World War I; amalgamated with dissident Socialists they later launched the Fascist movement.

The Risorgimento

Although a few grumbled, Italy settled down under the new order decreed by the Congress of Vienna of 1814-15. In the northeast, eastern Friuli, Trieste, Istria, and Trent were incorporated into the Austrian empire. The former republic of Venice and duchy of Milan formed the Lombard-Venetian kingdom of which the Austrian emperor was king. It was garrisoned by Austrian troops and administered by Austrian officials. The grand-duchy of Tuscany and the duchies of Parma and Modena were ruled despotically by relatives of the Austrian emperor. The theocratic papal states were re-established in their traditional boundaries and were ruled by Pius VII, back from his semi-imprisonment in France. Victor Emmanuel I of Savoy returned to Turin and added the former republic of Genoa to his Sardinian kingdom. In 1816 the Bourbon Ferdinand IV of Naples and Sicily became Ferdinand I, king of the Two Sicilies. Another Bourbon was duke of Lucca.

As before 1796, only more so, Austria was the paramount power in Italy. There was, however, a difference. This was no longer the Austria of the reforming Hapsburg-Lorraine princes. It was the traditionalist Austria of Francis II and of his chief minister Metternich: politically despotic, religiously intolerant, intellectually conformist, economically stagnant. For nearly four decades, from 1809 to 1848, Metternich was the main power in the Austrian dominions and a major influence in European continental affairs. With its violence, its Jacobin Terror, its wars which lasted for twenty-three years, the French Revolution had terrorized both European traditionalists and moderate reformers. As Metternich saw it, Austria's function was first and foremost to prevent a recurrence of what had happened between 1789 and 1815. It was her duty, particularly in Italy and Germany, to enforce internal order; and everywhere in Europe to maintain peace. Alexander I of Russia, founder of the Holy Alliance, committed in the name of Christian principles to the enforcement of order and peace, agreed with Metternich's program.

When the second period of Austrian domination began most Italians were traditionalists: the overwhelming majority of the two privileged classes and the working classes, a smaller majority of the middle classes. Traditionalists were attached to the past, opposed to innovation of any kind, deeply loyal to the institutions of the absolute state, convinced that authoritarianism is the best guarantee of order and happiness. Resentful of the French, hating any kind of revolution, they were relieved when Hapsburg-Lorraine and Bourbon and Savoy princes and the pope returned to their capitals. Clericalism, the all-pervading intellectual and political influence of the clergy, was the bulwark of traditionalism.

Traditionalists agreed that the ignorance of obedient and poor masses is preferable to the enlightenment of free and prosperous citizens. But they miscalculated: masses that are ignorant are also apathetic, and in 1859-60 their apathy favored the success of the nation's liberal minority. This minority was recruited almost exclusively from the intelligentsia. In 1815, liberals were more numerous than their forerunners, the admirers of the French Revolution, had been in 1796. Their program was that of contemporary British and French reformers, and it justified the traditionalists' contention that liberals wanted to introduce "foreign" ideas and institutions.

There were differences among the liberals; these had already come into the open during the short period of French-sponsored Italian republics of 1796-99. Right-wingers, or moderates, favored constitutional parliamentarian regimes based on limited suffrage, under a hereditary monarch. On the national level they favored federalism. They read Locke and Voltaire. The left-wingers, or radicals, started from a generous concept of man's innate goodness and put equality and justice on a level with liberty. Intolerant of limitations to national sovereignty, they opposed checks and balances, wanted universal suffrage and, on the national level, a unitary state. They read Rousseau and Bentham. As time went on, "liberal" came to denote the moderates only (including Catholic neo-Guelphs of the 1840's). The left-wingers were republicans and democrats. Divided on their concept of man and of political institutions, moderates and radicals were equally patriotic and equally opposed to foreign domination and traditionalism.

The upheaval caused by the French domination did not subside completely when the Austrians returned and traditional authorities were reinstated. In addition to the freemasonry and the *carboneria*, a number of smaller clandestine revolutionary groups were at work. Between 1817 and 1832 there were many conspiracies, a few revolts, and three uprisings: one in Naples in 1820, another in the Piedmont area of the kingdom of Sardinia in 1821, a third in the Romagna district of the papal states and in the duchy of Modena, in 1831. The conspiracies, revolts, and uprisings were not the prelude to a new era, they were the end of the great French revolutionary storm. They all failed. Austrian repression, through military intervention in Naples, Piedmont, Modena, and Romagna, through routine police action in the Lombard-Venetian kingdom, was swift and efficient. Executioners were kept busy. Prisons were full. Order and peace prevailed.

Not so much linked to the French Revolution, more Italian, was the action of the generation that achieved maturity in the 1830's and 1840's and saw the unification of most of the country in 1859-60. Fearful of repercussions from the July 1830 revolution in France, the Sardinian authorities increased their vigilance. At the end of that year, their attention was caught by, among others, a young intellectual of twenty-five, Giuseppe Mazzini, and a twenty-year-old aristocrat, Camillo Benso di Cavour. Mazzini was arrested and spent three months in prison. He later went into exile in France and Switzerland, then eventually settled in Great Britain. Cavour, a junior officer in the Sardinian army, was transferred under semi-arrest to an isolated fortress. After resigning his commission, he withdrew to the country, taking over the management of a family estate, studying economics, following political events closely, and later promoting banking and industrial enterprises. Mazzini and Cavour never met. One became the leader of the Italian republican democrats, the other of liberal moderates. Working on different levels and through different means, they played equal roles in promoting the unification of the country.

Dissatisfied with freemasonry and *carboneria*, late in 1831 Mazzini organized the secret society *Giovane Italia* (Young Italy). The society promoted an uprising in 1833 which failed. One of the members who escaped arrest and went into exile in Belgium was the thirty-two-year-old priest Vincenzo Gioberti, later a leader of progressive Catholics. A second rising was organized by Young Italy in 1834. This too failed, and another to escape into exile was the twenty-seven-year old Giuseppe Garibaldi. A guerrilla fighter against dictatorships in Latin America, defender of the short-lived Roman democratic republic in 1849, he led The Thousand who conquered the Two Sicilies in 1860, thus ending the political division between southern Italy and the rest of the country. Twelve years older than Mazzini was Mastai-Ferretti, who became Pope Pius IX in 1846 and who, as a bishop, had rescued a few young revolutionaries involved in the 1831 uprising. Among these was Louis Napoleon Bonaparte, nephew of Napoleon. Louis Napoleon was elected president of the French republic at the end of 1848. He was responsible for the fall of the Roman republic in 1849, and as Emperor Napoleon III played the major role in events leading to the end of Austrian domination in Italy in 1859 and the following years. Ten years younger than Cavour was Victor Emmanuel of Savoy, who succeeded to the Sardinian throne in 1849, loyally supported his prime minister Cavour in the 1850's, and became king of Italy in 1861.

The Mazzinian conspiracies of 1833 and 1834 were followed by many others. Mazzini was an inspirer of men, a prophet, not a statesman or an organizer. The conspiracies failed. Austrian power, clericalism, and traditionalism were strongly entrenched in Italy—or so it seemed. Then the unexpected happened. A nearly bloodless revolution in Paris led to the proclamation of a republic in France in February 1848. Everywhere on the continent liberals, democrats, and patriots were jubilant. Demonstrations led to a revolution in Vienna in March. Old Metternich fled. There were agitations, demonstrations, uprisings, and revolutions in Hungary, in Germany, in Italy: the vast area between France and Russia, of which Vienna had been the political capital since 1815. Italian sovereigns granted constitutions. Successful popular uprisings expelled Austrian garrisons from Milan, Venice, and other cities in March. In response to an appeal from Milan, and pressed by his own new liberal government, King Charles Albert of Sardinia (who in his youth had been sympathetic to the *carbonari*) declared war against Austria. There was great enthusiasm among Italian liberals—a minority unaware that the masses (with few exceptions, as in Milan) were not interested in liberalism, constitutionalism, unification.

The liberals forced the governments of the Two Sicilies, the papal states, and Tuscany to join Sardinia in the war against Austria. Successes were short-lived. At the end of April 1848 Pope Pius IX declared that he could not take part in the war against the Catholic Austrian empire, and withdrew his troops. The clerical majority of the Catholics rejoiced, the progressive minority became uncertain. Counting on the loyalty of the Neapolitan masses, Ferdinand II of the Two Sicilies suspended the constitution in May. The political crisis had not affected the Austrian armed forces, loyal to their emperor and to the traditional way of life which he personified. Generals took the initiative in re-establishing the emperor's authority. The Sardinian troops were defeated in the summer of 1848 and again in 1849 after a six-month armistice. Charles Albert of Sardinia abdicated and was replaced by his son Victor Emmanuel II.

The moderates' failure spurred the democrats who proclaimed republics in Tuscany, Rome, and Venice, led respectively by Guerrazzi, Mazzini, and Manin. The pitiful volunteer forces raised amid the indifference of most of the population could not stop the Austrians, who occupied Tuscany in May 1849 and captured Venice at the end of August, nor the French who came to re-establish papal authority and to whom Rome surrendered early in July. The first war of the *Risorgimento* was over. The police were working hard to eliminate revolutionary tendencies in the areas directly controlled by Austria, in the Two Sicilies, and in the papal states.

After 1849, however, there was a difference, one that made for a national climate vastly unlike that of 1814-1847. Victor Emmanuel II rejected the Austrian request that constitutional liberties be abolished in the kingdom of Sardinia. Here there was some freedom—political and intellectual. Initiatives could be taken, plans could be made: not just by deputies and ministers, but also by citizens and by tens of thousands of exiles who had come from all over Italy to Turin and Genoa, the two main cities of the kingdom of Sardinia. To the exiles, in particular to Manin who had led the Venetian republic, was due the formation in 1856 of the National Society, which aimed at the unification of Italy under Victor Emmanuel II. The National Society included moderates willing to renounce federalism and democrats willing to renounce republicanism, in favor of constitutional unitarianism under a Savoy king. The hopes of the Italian patriots were focused on Sardinia.

Cavour was soon to gain distinction in the Sardinian parliament. In 1852 he became prime minister. Enlightened fiscal policies, political stability, and governmental stimulus to economic activities quickly made the continental regions of the kingdom of Sardinia the most advanced section of Italy. Internal administration was made more efficient, ecclesiastical privilege was curbed (as a result Cavour was excommunicated), public education was improved, railroads were built. Most important of all was the reorganization of the armed forces. Cavour was able to convince parliament and the king in 1855 that Sardinia should join Great Britain and France in the war being waged in the Crimea to check Russian expansion toward the Mediterranean. Sardinia could now count on the support of France's imperial government and of British public opinion (which moreover was shocked by police excesses in the Two Sicilies, publicized by Gladstone). In parliament, Cavour achieved the liberal coalition of progressive moderates and unitarian democrats which, outside parliament, had given birth to the National Society.

The second war of the *Risorgimento* resulted from French dynamism. Supported by a majority of the French nation and entrusted with dictatorial powers, Emperor Napoleon III aimed at re-establishing the leadership of France in Europe. Successful against Russia, Napoleon turned his eyes toward Italy. Late in 1857 he let Cavour know that he would help Sardinia if there were a war to expel the Austrians from Italy. His goal was to substitute French influence for Austrian. Cavour and Italian liberals had other plans; their aim was to unite as much of Italy as possible. However, they could not do this alone. In 1858 Cavour met Napoleon secretly. In April 1859 the Austrian government fell into a trap prepared by Cavour, and declared war on Sardinia. A strong French army crossed the Alps. The French were victorious, but after a short campaign Napoleon, frightened by Catholic opposition in France and by rumors of Prussian mobilization, signed an armistice with the Austrians. It added Lombardy to the kingdom of Sardinia.

The landslide had begun. There were revolutions in the smaller states of Tuscany, Modena, and Parma and in the four Romagna provinces of the papal states. Provisional governments headed by members of the National Society asked to be annexed by Sardinia. Cavour bought French approval in March 1860 by ceding French-speaking districts of the Sardinian state to France. He counted on the support of Great Britain where, in 1859, a pro-Italian Liberal majority had replaced the pro-Austrian Conservative one in the House of Commons. The smaller states were added to Sardinia. In May 1860, Garibaldi and a thousand secretly recruited volunteers sailed from Quarto near Genoa toward Sicily, with money and weapons supplied by the Sardinian government. Conveniently and discreetly helped in various crucial moments by the British navy, and by British diplomacy which discouraged intervention in favor of the king of the Two Sicilies, Garibaldi entered Naples early in September. In the same month, Sardinian troops occupied ten more provinces of the papal states; only Rome and its district remained to the pope, a protégé of French Catholics. On March 17, 1861, the first Italian parliament proclaimed the kingdom of Italy. On June 6 Cavour died, in his fifty-second year.

Venice and Rome and their districts remained outside the new Italian state; so did the small districts of northeast Italy directly administered from Vienna. Prussian initiative enabled Italy to incorporate Venice and Rome. Chancellor of Prussia since the end of 1862,

Bismarck aimed at eliminating Austrian influence from Germany. The defeat of the Austrians by the Prussians during the Seven Weeks' War of 1866 gave Venice to Italy—Prussia's ally. Four years later, in August 1870, the French, involved in a war with Prussia, withdrew their troops from Rome. The French were defeated by the Prussians early in September, and on the twentieth of that month Italian troops entered Rome. The age of foreign domination had ended, and with it the political division of Italy and the temporal power of the papacy. The tenacity of a few, the courage of a patriotic minority, and the vicissitudes of European power politics had, in 1859-70, replaced small regional states with varying degrees of dependency to foreign powers with an independent Italian state.

After Unification: A Slow Start

Americans would describe the new Italian state as conservative. For Italians, compared with the authoritarian traditionalism dominant since the sixteenth century (and with the Fascist state that replaced it in 1922) it was liberal. Suffrage was limited: in 1861 there were about half a million voters in a population of a little over twenty-two million. But the introduction of limited suffrage where there had been none was a greater revolution than the extensions of the suffrage in 1881, 1912, and 1919 and the granting of universal suffrage in 1946. Divided into an elected House and an appointed Senate, parliament occupied the center of the political scene. The Sardinian constitution of 1848, which became the Italian constitution of 1861, gave the king considerable powers. But within a short time the executive became subject to the legislative power. When Humbert I succeeded his father Victor Emmanuel II in 1878, Italy had a parliamentary government.

Had it been founded on universal suffrage, the new Italian state could easily have reverted to authoritarianism. The parliamentary system, and everything that went with it, survived at first largely because the Catholic majority was instructed by the pope (who had resented the loss of the papal states) not to take part in political activities. So except for supporting some guerrillas in the south, the Catholics did not actively oppose the new state. As the believers among the minority entitled to vote obeyed the papal injunction, a free hand was left to Liberals, Democrats and, later, Socialists, who were antagonistic to each other but all equally opposed to clericalism. By the time the papal injunction was rescinded, in 1918, clericalism had lost ground, and many Italian Catholics supported the position now described as Christian Democratic.

Parliamentarianism was the key to many changes. Local authorities acquired considerable autonomy and responsibility. Freedom of teaching and lay instruction in public schools replaced the former rigid ecclesiastical supervision of all educational activities. In 1861 three adults out of four were illiterate, in some southern areas nine out of ten. After unification, public elementary education became free and there were efforts to make it universal. De facto separation of Church and state curbed clericalism. Freedom of conscience replaced the monopoly enforced by the Catholic clergy since the Counter Reformation. (Italy was the first European nation to have practicing Jews in its government.) Through a free press, new ideas were formulated, discussed, and circulated. Freedom of association, at first limited, soon expanded. One national free market replaced many regulated and protected markets. Freedom of contract increased the mobility of capital. The ecclesiastical mortmain, previously weighing heavily on the Italian economy, was abolished. An attempt was made to have as much free trade as possible with other nations. Economic initiative grew.

The unification of Italy was a political revolution. The real revolution—the transformation of a way of life resulting from changing ideas, values, and attitudes—was slow in coming. In class insolence and servility, male arrogance and female docility, the authoritarian way of life persisted. In 1861 a considerable gulf separated the traditionalist majority of the nation from the ruling minority. That gulf narrowed gradually, but was far from closed when World War I began. The gulf explains the contrast between what happened at two different levels for several decades. At the level of public activities the state, governed and administered by the minority, was at least relatively efficient. At the level of private activities, the nation tended instead to be stagnant or at best to progress slowly. For a generation or so after unification, the Italian nation did not produce the spurt of energy characteristic of, for instance, the German nation which, unified in 1866-71, had immediately made great strides in all fields of endeavor. Taking economic data as an index, the gap between the

Italian nation and the nations of northwestern Europe was greater in 1890 than in 1861. Even Russia progressed faster than Italy.

Many responsible Italians assumed that institutional homogeneity would automatically bring national cohesion. In the 1860's it seemed therefore that the major problem facing the new Italian state was the creation of a homogeneous bureaucratic structure, no longer Piedmontese, Neapolitan, or Tuscan, but Italian. This one problem, however, involved most aspects of public activities: integration of administrative personnel, enactment of new legal codes and reorganization of the judiciary, complete overhaul of fiscal policies, amalgamation of the armed forces. Then there were other problems the state had to face: lack of economic infrastructure, particularly in relation to communications and sources of energy; general lack of confidence in the stability of the new state, and consequent immobility of the scant available capital; illiteracy; poor health conditions with high incidence of many diseases and lack of doctors and hospitals. To these was added—as soon as the initial shock of Garibaldi's easy conquest was over—the pro-Bourbon *jacquerie* in the peninsular south. This peasant uprising led to many years of guerrilla warfare, costly in human and in financial terms. Then, in the 1860's, there were the conspiratorial raids of Italian patriots aimed at liberating Venice and Rome. The raids could have involved Italy in serious international complications, and therefore had to be repressed. Later came the nationalist agitation for the liberation of Austrian Trent and Trieste.

For about thirty years after 1861 the politically active section of the restricted Italian electorate was fairly homogeneous. The two main parties in parliament differed about as much as British Conservatives and Liberals—that is, their differences were in degree more than in kind. These two parties were the *Destra* (Right) of moderates, who after the death of Cavour in 1861 became more and more conservative, and the *Sinistra* (Left) of democrats, who gradually moved from the left to the center. The Right had a parliamentary majority from 1861 to 1876, the Left from 1876 to 1891. The Right wanted a strong centralized bureaucracy, limited suffrage, considerable autonomy for the executive branch, separation of Church and state but respect for ecclesiastical authority, sound fiscal policies founded on a balanced budget, as much aloofness as possible in international affairs, an efficient military establishment. The Left wanted wider (but not universal) suffrage, bureaucratic decentralization, subordination of the executive to the legislative power, straightforward anti-Church policies, compulsory lay universal education at the elementary level, a decrease of the heavy fiscal burden even at the cost of an unbalanced budget, international free trade, and a dynamic foreign policy aimed at increasing Italian influence in international affairs. The combined electorate of Right and Left accounted for less than 4 per cent of the adult population in the 1860's, and about 10 per cent in the 1880's.

During its fifteen years in power (1861-1876) the Right achieved the integration of the bureaucracy, the judiciary, and the armed forces; improved the economic infrastructure (for instance in 1876 there were 5,000 miles of railroads, against 1,000 in 1861) and balanced the budget; laid the foundation of a sound public school system; and ended the southern *jacquerie*, at the cost of many thousand lives. Centrifugal forces were checked; age-long differences among Italians and regional particularism began to weaken. The Right tried to solve the thorny problem of Church-state relationships with the Law of Guarantees of 1871. The law was not accepted by the papacy, which did not renounce its claims to the former papal states until the Lateran agreements of 1929 with Italy's Fascist government. In external affairs, the alliance with Prussia against Austria led to the brief third war of the *Risorgimento* in 1866. Italian defeats were compensated for by Prussian victories, and Venetia was added to the Italian kingdom. Neutrality during the Franco-Prussian war of 1870-71 brought Rome and Latium to Italy. Except for the Prussian alliance Italy, at odds with her two powerful neighbors, Austria and France, was diplomatically isolated.

During its fifteen years of power (1876-1891) the Left widened the suffrage; abolished taxes weighing heavily on the poor; introduced some social legislation (insurance against accident, protection of women and children in factories); improved the public school system; abolished ecclesiastical tithes and compulsory religious instruction; promoted the establishment of a large number of savings and cooperative banks which stimulated industrial development; enacted greatly improved legal codes; strengthened the military forces. The cabinets of the Left, and the parliamentary majority which supported them, abandoned their free trade principles, and in 1887 introduced full-scale protectionism, using Alexander Hamilton's infant industries argument to justify their action.

The Left's dynamism in international affairs meant, in practical terms, alliances and colonialism. Since 1871, the main aim of the German chancellor Bismarck had been the consolidation of peace in Europe through a system of German-centered alliances, and the isolation of France, still reputedly the most aggressive European nation. Bismarck's support for Austrian claims in the Balkans in 1878 had led by 1879 to an alliance between the two central European empires. To a growing number of Italians to be anti-Austrian, now that Italy was unified, seemed a thing of the past. Some in responsible positions, including the minister of foreign affairs, hoped that in time German pressure and compensations in the Balkans would induce Austria to surrender Italian-speaking border districts. The establishment of a French protectorate in Tunisia in 1881 caused deep emotion in Italy, where it was interpreted as a threat to Italian sovereignty. Italian trade with both Germany and Austria was increasing, and greater economic collaboration appealed to many. Playing on these various elements, Bismarck's able diplomacy induced Italy to join the Austro-German alliance. (The Triple Alliance, as it was called, was renewed several times and lasted until denounced by Italy on May 3, 1915.) Italian relations with Great Britain, then the world's major power, remained consistently good.

Great Britain was the channel through which the colonial ambitions of the Italian Left were first realized. A British invitation in 1882 to intervene jointly in Egypt, where a number of Europeans had been massacred by Arab nationalists, was rejected by the Italian government which, however, annexed Assab on the Red Sea, vaguely an Egyptian possession since the 1820's. The British suggestion that Italy help check the fanatical slave-raiding followers of a Moslem prophet then devastating the Sudan led to the Italian occupation in 1885 of Massaua, also on the Red Sea, and of its hinterland belonging to Ethiopia. Intervention in an Ethiopian civil war led to the treaty of Uccially of 1889 which—in its Italian version somewhat different from the Amharic—established Italy's protectorate over Ethiopia. In the same year an Italian protectorate was also established over two small Somali areas southeast of Ethiopia.

Growing National Dynamism

By the end of the nineteenth century, the generation born between the 1840's and 1860's was setting the tone for the nation. The torpor inherited from long foreign and ecclesiastical domination began to break, even among the lower middle class, the urban proletariat, and the peasantry, who with few exceptions had remained passive during the struggle for independence and free institutions. Statesmen like Giolitti and leaders of new movements like the Socialist Turati, the Christian Democrat Murri, and the Nationalist Corradini were influenced by passions different from those that had inspired the previous generation. Under the stimulus of figures as varied as the poet and novelist D'Annunzio, the scientist Marconi, the philosopher Croce, Italian intellectual life became less provincial. With energetic and imaginative entrepreneurs at work, the economic life of the country had new vitality. In the late 1880's, the first large-scale industrial enterprises were established for the production of steel, chemicals, and electricity. Textile and mechanical industries were expanding rapidly, chiefly in northwestern Italy. Landowners were increasing agricultural yield by adopting techniques developed in advanced countries like Great Britain—for example, crop rotation, selective breeding, and rational use of fertilizers.

In the early 1890's the extreme conservatives lost their representation in parliament, and the distinction between Right and Left became more and more blurred until the two groups merged informally; the process of merging was known as *trasformismo*. The Liberals, as members of this new grouping were called, had a majority in parliament until the elections of 1919, and governed the country until the Fascist *coup d'état* of 1922. They were divided into numerous groups, of which the largest and most influential was the center, headed by Giolitti, prime minister first in 1892-93 and for the last time in 1920-21. For thirty years Giolitti was the most authoritative figure in Italian politics. In the 1890's, with an enlarged electorate, the *Estrema* (extreme Left) gained ground. This was composed of intransigent Republicans and Socialists, still undecided between dictatorial absolutism and parliamentarian liberty. Between the Liberals and the *Estrema* were the Radicals, whose progressivism was centered on individual liberty: this put them ideologically closer to their Liberal opponents than to their Socialist allies. (Italian Radicals had a position akin to that of American New Deal Democrats in the 1930's.) In the 1913 elections, based on almost universal male suffrage, to the right of the Liberals appeared antiparliamentarian Nationalists, and (through partial ecclesiastical dispensation) Catholic deputies, wavering between authoritarianism and parliamentarianism.

The 1890's were an agitated decade. The awakening that had been expected but had not materialized in the 1860's was taking place a generation later. It led to awareness of social problems: there was enough economic expansion and improvement in standards of living to shake people from traditional torpor, and not enough to fulfill the expectations of the aroused masses. The excessive fluctuations that were a feature of capitalism in its early, unorganized phase led to greater economic instability and personal insecurity, for many, than had the previous stagnant economy. Failure and bankruptcy were common: they meant financial ruin for investors and hungry unemployment for wage-earners and their families. At the same time working people were becoming aware that a different and better life existed, and they felt they were entitled to a share of it. Large-scale emigration had begun, mostly from southern Italy and Sicily, to the United States and the southernmost Latin American republics. Emigration relieved some of the economic pressure in Italy; it also increased dissatisfaction among those who compared America with Italy.

What in the 1870's and 1880's isolated revolutionaries like the anarchist Cafiero and the socialist Costa had begun, became in the 1890's a large-scale extremist movement of social protest. Middle-class intellectuals (Labriola, Turati, Ferri, and many others) inspired their followers to organize labor unions among factory workers and agricultural laborers and, in 1892, to found a Marxist Socialist party. Anarchists agitated: Italian anarchists were responsible for the assassination of King Humbert I of Italy in 1900, and also of a president of the French republic, an Austrian empress, and a Spanish prime minister. There were demonstrations and strikes which led, particularly in 1893 and 1898, to bloody battles between strikers and public forces. This happened in the lower Po valley and in Sicily, where Socialists organized workers' *Fasci* (unions), a term later resurrected by subversive extreme Nationalists, the Fascists.

Hampered by the unfounded commonplaces of classical economists, as much as by the vested interests of the enfranchised minority, ministers and deputies of the 1890's dealt ineptly with economic and social problems. The Radicals, who counted the distinguished economist De Viti De Marco among their leaders, proposed measures along the lines of the American New Deal of the 1930's; however, they were not numerous enough in parliament to carry weight. A serious defeat inflicted on the Italians in 1896 by the Ethiopians, whose Amharic version of the 1889 treaty did not mention a protectorate, caused deep feeling in Italy. These were difficult years. Some thought it a miracle that Italy did not revert to despotism during this period. Helping to keep this from happening was the diversity of the opposition, which included such incompatible groups as Clericals, Nationalists, Republicans, and a variety of collectivists: Socialists, Syndicalists, anarchists. Also helping was the fact that both the labor movement and the most influential opposition group on the extreme left, the Marxist Socialists, were poorly organized. Not a miracle, but a sign of political maturity, was the sense of responsibility of deputies who were able to put aside the antagonism between Right and Left of the previous decades and to unite in 1900-1903 as Liberals.

The murder in June 1900 of King Humbert I, a mediocre but good man, shocked all Italians. The shock probably helped mend the situation enough to ensure internal order and therefore progress. Many leftist revolutionaries were appalled by this senseless act of violence. The problem of whether to advocate dictatorship or parliamentary procedure, force or legal action, seriously divided Italian Socialists, many of whom discovered that they were democrats rather than collectivists. At the other end of the political rainbow, many Catholics came to the conclusion that a parliamentary regime was preferable to a subversive dictatorship. Leo XIII expressed approval of democracy provided it was Christian democracy, defined early in 1903 as the paternal concern of the rulers for the welfare of the people. Pius X, in view of the 1904 elections, authorized a limited participation of Catholics (as voters only, not as candidates or as a party) in the Italian political arena, in order to prevent the subversion of the social order. After the king's assassination Zanardelli, a survivor of the first war of the *Risorgimento* and leader of the former Left, now a

Liberal, became prime minister. He was soon succeeded by Giolitti who, with the support of a strong parliamentary majority, remained prime minister until the spring of 1914 except for two brief periods when the premiership was held by other Liberal leaders.

Liberals of this last pre–World War I period, which began with Victor Emmanuel's accession to the throne in 1900, had inherited from the Right of the 1861-1891 generation an attachment to parliamentarianism and a fondness for sound finance. From the Left of the same generation they had inherited a program of gradual reform, aiming at greater equality among citizens and greater prosperity. As a whole they were moderately progressive. During those fourteen years a major Liberal goal was the gradual democratization of the Italian state. This could be achieved only by inducing hostile sections of the population to accept parliamentarianism as the foundation of the political process.

The dispute within the Socialist party between advocates of violence and dictatorship and advocates of legality and democratic procedure ended in 1908 with the defeat of the former. Authoritarian socialism was still strong, but less so than before. A wing of the Socialist movement, the forerunners of the Social Democrats of today, not only accepted democratic procedure but was also willing to cooperate on the government level with non-Socialists: in Marxist terminology, with bourgeois parties. Members of this wing, including Bonomi (who was prime minister in 1921-22 and again in 1944-45), left the Socialist party in 1912. The 1904 relaxation of papal political directives, already mentioned, was followed by the 1913 agreement sponsored by ecclesiastical authorities, which allowed Catholics and Liberals to vote for the same candidates. Nationalists were becoming ever more numerous among the educated classes, but only a minority of them supported the authoritarian Nationalist party when it was founded in 1910. The Liberal policy was to make clear to the opposition groups that the political liberty of which parliamentarianism is the key was advantageous to all. On this basis Liberals, led by Giolitti, acceded to the request of democratic Socialists, Republicans, and Radicals for universal male suffrage; to the Catholics' request for a relaxation of anticlericalism and better relations with the papacy; to the Nationalists' request for a new round of colonial expansion. Liberal Italy was becoming the Italians' Italy. With the electoral reform of 1912, all sectors of the Italian nation could participate in the political process.

There still was considerable subversive agitation in 1900-1914, down to the revolutionary riots of June 1914 led by the anarchist Malatesta, in which a role was played by the future Socialist leader and vice-premier (1963-65) Nenni. The riots were quelled without the bloody excesses that had characterized repressions of similar events in 1893 and 1898. There were many strikes, and the Italian Confederation of Labor (suppressed by the Fascists in 1926, reorganized in 1943) was established in 1906. But despite their leaders' public utterances, the strikers' goals were more economic than political.

Political agitation did not prevent increasing numbers of citizens from working more efficiently. The real value of agricultural output doubled in the eighteen years preceding Italy's entry into World War I. Capital invested in industrial corporations increased five-fold. The number of industrial enterprises rose in 1900-1914 from 117,000 to 244,000, and that of industrial wage-earners from one and one-third million to two and one-third million. Foreign trade nearly doubled between 1900 and 1910. German, Swiss, Belgian investments, entrepreneurship, and managerial efficiency stimulated the Italian economy. Emigration was often deplored, but emigrants' remittances (especially from Italians in the United States) covered most of the deficit in the balance of trade. The insistence on sound currency, financial solvency, and a balanced budget was not a hindrance to the realization of important public works. Railroads, nationalized in 1905, were extended; marshes were reclaimed in the lower Po valley; aqueducts were built, ports and harbors modernized, and useful public buildings erected. Illiteracy was cut in half; public education was expanded and made compulsory until the age of twelve. The health ministry successfully checked age-old diseases like pellagra and malaria. Social security was improved, cooperatives encouraged, emigrants helped. A government labor council, established in 1906, acted as intermediary between labor unions and parliament. By 1914 much still remained to be done to reach the distant goal of a democratic society. But a great deal had already been accomplished.

Foreign policy proved to be the Achilles' heel of the Liberal state. Giolitti and his supporters, basically opposed to military adventures, did not foresee the final outcome of an initiative they took in 1911 to appease Italian Nationalists. Agreements of the Left government with Germany and Austria in 1882, and in 1890 with Great Britain, as well as later agreements in 1900 with France and Russia, had recognized Italian claims to occupy two large, desertic African provinces of the Ottoman empire, Tripolitania and Cyrenaica (now forming the kingdom of Libya). This action was part of the dividing of inefficiently governed Moslem areas among dynamic Christian nations, in process since the middle of the eighteenth century.

In September 1911 Italy declared war on the Ottoman empire, disrupted since 1908 by a series of revolutions, counterrevolutions, uprisings, and *coups d'état*. It was not much of a war. The two provinces were occupied in October. In March 1912, Italian forces occupied Rhodes and a few other Aegean islands that had belonged to the Ottoman empire since 1522. It had all seemed very easy. But it was only a beginning. Taking advantage of Turkish defeats in the war with Italy, in 1912 four small Balkan states attacked the Ottoman possessions in Europe and won a victory. In 1913 they fought each other to divide the spoils. These were the first and second Balkan wars. Austrian fear of an enlarged Serbian state on Austria's southern border, and the assassination of the Austrian crown prince by a Serbian nationalist, led to a series of declarations of war between July 28 and August 6, 1914. World War I was on: the process of democratizing Italian institutions and liberalizing the Italian way of life was to be interrupted for thirty years.

EIGHT

THE CRISIS OF 1914-1922

World War I was a turning point for Italy, as it was for many other European nations. In Italy it is still called the Great War. Even if later generations felt that their predecessors had exaggerated the importance of this war and its impact on national life, it did bring enormous change.

The war and postwar crises ended the predominance of the Liberal minority, which for a hundred years had set the tone for the nation —first as opposition, and later as ruling class. By 1914 more and more Italians of all classes were groping for new institutions and a different way of life. Some were looking for a modernized version of Catholic-centered traditionalism, the opponent defeated by the Liberals in the nineteenth century. Many Italians were Socialists, a term which had a wider meaning then than it does today, since it included those who later seceded to form the Communist party, as well as extinct or semi-extinct movements like syndicalism and anarchism. Still others, moved by a sincere nationalistic obsession, joined the postwar fringe Socialists with whom they shared hatred for the Liberal state, and found their home in fascism.

World War I

During the forty days of 1914 between the murder of the Austrian Crown Prince and the declarations of war of Austria, Germany, Russia, France, and Great Britain, there was as much tension in Italy as in the other European great powers. Italy had been the ally of

Germany and Austria-Hungary since 1882. Considering that Italians
were traditionally antagonistic to the Germans, that a French victory
over Austria in 1859 had made possible the unification of the country, and that there had been another war against Austria in 1866, the
1882 alliance would seem an expression of the irrational in history.
In reality it was, rather, an expression of historical continuity. Since
the middle of the eighth century, when the Frankish Pepin III invaded Italy and created the papal states, relations between the Italians and the French had more often been bad than good. Since the
middle of the tenth century, when the German Otto I was crowned
king of Italy and emperor of a renewed Western Roman Empire, Italy
had often been linked to Germany.

In the years immediately preceding World War I, the Triple Alliance between Austria-Hungary, Germany, and Italy had been weakened by agreements with Great Britain and by a rapprochement with
France. Two main factors were behind these developments. There
was *irredentismo*, the agitation of Italian patriots clamoring for the
annexation of Austro-Hungarian border districts inhabited by Italians:
the Trentino, the city of Trieste, and areas near Trieste. There was
the awareness on the part of responsible Italians of the change in the
European balance of power: Germany's economic progress and national efficiency and discipline had made the German empire the
strongest military power in the world. The situation of 1914 was vastly
different from that of a few decades earlier, when France was supposed to be the strongest military power and Great Britain was the
wealthiest state.

In July 1914 a small minority of Italians (mainly the authoritarian
Nationalists) wanted to intervene in the war on the side of Germany.
Another small minority (democratic Radicals and Republicans)
wanted intervention on the side of the Allies, in whom they saw the
defenders of democracy against aggressive German militarism. A still
smaller minority (Marxist and Syndicalist revolutionary Socialists)
favored any sort of intervention in the hope, expressed by Lenin and
his Bolsheviki, of transforming the "capitalistic" war into a "revolutionary" or class war. Most Italians of all classes were against intervention: Liberals because of their conviction that neutrality would
bring greater economic and political gains than war, Socialists because

of their pacifism and internationalism, Catholics because both France and Austria-Hungary were predominantly Catholic. Taking advantage of a clause in the 1882 treaty of alliance, on August 3, 1914 the Italian government, supported by a parliamentary majority, decided on non-intervention.

Official and nonofficial Allied and German agents soon got busy in Italy. The Allies, especially the French, were the more persuasive. French Nationalists convinced leaders of the Italian Nationalist party that their first duty was the liberation of Trent and Trieste. French Socialists induced some Italian Socialists to come out in favor of the Allies. Among them was the young editor of the official Socialist newspaper L'Avanti, Benito Mussolini, then known as a left-wing or revolutionary Socialist. Violent pro-Allied manifestations organized by Nationalists on the right and by democrats and revolutionaries on the left increased, stimulating patriotism and scaring neutralists who, as men of peace, found it difficult to answer violence with violence. Inflammatory speeches were made by exiles from Trent and Trieste. Leading intellectuals spoke for intervention. By the spring of 1915 the neutralist majority, in parliament and among the public, had the defeatist attitude of those who feel that the times are against them.

Giolitti, leader of the center Liberals and a convinced neutralist, resigned on questions of internal policies and was succeeded as prime minister by Salandra. Leader of the nationalistically inclined right-wing Liberals, Salandra headed a shaky parliamentary majority. His foreign minister, the former premier Sonnino (also a right-wing Liberal) asked the Austro-Hungarian government for territorial concessions which the Austrians, against German advice, rejected. French and British diplomats instead promised vast territorial gains if Italy would side with the Allies: Trentino and Trieste, the German-speaking area of the Tyrol south of the Alpine divide, eastern Friuli, Istria and most of Dalmatia where the population was mainly Slavic, and coastal districts of Albania. Later, Italy was also promised a share in the division of the Ottoman empire and additions to her African colonies, should Germany lose her colonial possessions. A formal agreement was signed secretly in London on April 26, 1915. Early in May Italy denounced the Triple Alliance, and on May 23 sent an ultimatum to Austria-Hungary. Hostilities began on the twenty-fourth. As often happens when there is war or the threat of war, internal divisions subsided. Neutralism disappeared, and only the majority section of the Socialists refused to renounce their pacifism.

In the spring of 1915 few people in Italy foresaw the suffering, the disruption of economic activities, and the postwar tension the war would cause. The illusions of 1914 still persisted; leaders and public on both sides of the fence, with few exceptions, were convinced that the war would be a short one and that the major problems would be promptly settled at a peace conference. Recent experience seemed to rule out a long war. Actual fighting in the Italian-Turkish war of 1911, and the Balkan wars of 1912 and 1913, had lasted just a few weeks, with negligible casualties. People mistakenly relied on political maturity, economic interdependence, and widely diffused internationalism to halt hostilities after a short time. The generation that had enthusiastically greeted the two peace conferences of the Hague, in 1899 and 1907, and the establishment of the International Court of Arbitration, did not believe in war. People failed to take enough into account the depth of passions, the complexity of interests, the rigidity of institutions and thought existing at the time.

In 1916 they saw what war really meant: at Verdun, the Somme, the Isonzo; in Galicia and in the Balkans; on the high seas. More countries were drawn into the conflict. New means of destruction were employed: aircraft, submarines, poison gas (first used in 1915 by the Germans), and tanks (first used by the British in 1916). In 1917 the Allies experienced a year of despair with the collapse of Russia, the near breakdown of morale in France, the almost successful German submarine blockade of Great Britain. Italians had their share with the defeat of Caporetto, the loss of entire army corps, the enemy occupation of eastern Venetia. Without the weight of American intervention 1918 might well have been the year of German victory on the western front, as 1917 had been on the eastern front. Instead, the German spring offensive was stopped, and the summer offensive soon became a retreat. An Austro-Hungarian offensive in Italy failed, largely as the result of the presence of American troops. Allied morale rose. A French-led Allied offensive in the Balkans and a British offensive in the Middle East made Bulgaria and the Ottoman empire seek an armistice early in the autumn. In October 1918 the multinational Austro-Hungarian empire began to break up: Czech democrats took over in Prague, Croat (Yugoslav) nationalists in Zagreb, Hungarian republicans in Budapest. An Italian offensive begun early in October progressed speedily, and on November 4 the armistice of Villa Giusti ended hostilities on the Italian front. With the armistice of November 11 between Germany and the Allies, the bloodiest war ever fought came to an end.

Postwar Agitation

European nations reacted to the experience of World War I and to the postwar crisis more in relation to the level of their political maturity than to that of their sufferings or economic difficulties. In human and economic terms Italians had suffered fewer losses than the French, Germans, or British. But they were less prepared or less willing to face ordeals. Two years of leftist agitation were followed by a rightist subversive reaction which within another two years swept away the Liberal state.

Wartime discipline broke down after the armistice. An antiwar reaction set in. Mobs attacked returning officers and demonstrated against those who had favored intervention in 1915. The worsening of economic conditions caused tension to grow rapidly. Despite American and British loans, war expenditures had caused heavy inflation. Prices rose, commodities became scarce. Speculators made fortunes while people with modest fixed incomes became destitute. Unemployment increased: agricultural workers could go back to their farms, but soldiers who had been industrial workers had difficulty in finding jobs. Hundreds of thousands of young officers had had little or no training for civilian work, and war experiences made it hard for them to adapt to civilian life.

Government leaders seemed unable to deal with the worsening economic problem. As in the 1890's, this inability was not just the result of the pressure of vested interests. The chief reason was that economic clichés were being taken for granted by the ruling class, which was counting on the nonexistent self-regulating mechanism of the market to mend the disruption of economic life. Increasing numbers of Italians of all classes turned to the Socialists, who promised a cure for economic ills through collectivism, and whose pacifism in 1914-15 seemed to have been justified by the turn of events. Along with the strengthening of the Socialist party, labor organizations and

Socialist cooperatives were expanded. Socialist-led demonstrations, agitations, and strikes increased by leaps and bounds, further disrupting the country's already upset economic structure.

A new factor complicated the situation: the appearance of a Catholic party on the Italian political scene. Before the war ended, Pope Benedict XV had completed the work of Pius X in rescinding the order of their predecessor Pius IX forbidding Catholics to take part in Italian politics. An able priest, Luigi Sturzo, with friends who had been active for some time as spokesmen for a modernized Catholic position in political, economic, and social affairs, launched the Popular party early in 1919. The new party had the support of sectors of all classes, although it drew most of its leadership from the professional middle class and much of its electoral strength from the peasantry. It was essentially a confessional party, aiming at re-establishing the influence of Catholicism in fields of particular interest to the Church (education, family legislation, supervision of communications media, repression of non-Catholic or anti-Catholic propaganda, etc.). Cutting across class lines, it weakened the Liberals and Socialists. Although the founders and much of the leadership were democratically inclined, the Popular party included a variety of currents from authoritarian clericalism to near-revolutionary Catholic collectivism.

Elections took place in November 1919 on the basis of proportional representation, in a tense atmosphere caused by growing fear of a violent Socialist revolution. To understand the emotions and events of the time, one has to remember that most Western and Central European nations, including Italy, were deeply affected by the Russian Bolshevik revolution and by Communist uprisings in Germany, Hungary, and elsewhere. In the House of Deputies, Liberals dropped from 304 to fewer than 200, Socialists doubled from 78 to 156, the Popular party elected 100 deputies. Democrats (particularly the Radicals) also lost heavily, while rightist groups (Nationalists and others) gained seats. Socialists scored heavily in local elections: a third of all municipalities had Socialist administrations. On the whole there was remarkably little violence, but Socialist demonstrations and strikes increased rapidly after the elections. Socialist agitation reached its climax in September 1920 when the General Confederation of Labor called for a general strike. Workers took over a number of important factories in northern Italy, but the union leaders proved incapable of running them. From then on Socialist agitation subsided.

Three main factors prevented a seizure of power by the Socialist party. Chief of these was the paralyzing effect of the breach between revolutionary Socialists urging the use of violence and democratic Socialists favoring parliamentary procedure. This led, in January 1921, to a complete split, patterned on what had taken place the previous month in the French Socialist party. Most of the revolutionary Socialists, nearly a third of the total membership, seceded from the Socialist party and formed the Communist party. The second factor was the presence of the new Catholic party, which attracted large sections of the working classes, particularly the peasantry. The third was the progressive policy followed by the Liberals during the ministries led by Nitti and Giolitti, who did their best to avoid bloodshed and to meet some of the Socialists' demands.

By the end of 1920 the worst of the economic crisis was over, and the threat of a Socialist revolution in Italy had gone. But the fear of it, caused by two years of continual agitation and heightened by what was known of Bolshevik terrorism in Russia, remained. There was a strong anti-Socialist reaction in the two-thirds of the Italian nation that had neither joined the Socialist party nor felt sympathy for it; this favored the sudden growth of fascism, the new subversive movement.

Many new political groups emerged during the critical months following the end of World War I. Most disappeared without a trace; some others were absorbed by already established parties. One achieved immediate importance and became, as the Christian Democratic party, the dominant element in Italian life after World War II. Another, the *Fasci di Combattimento* (Fighting Unions), was successful a little later and ruled Italy from 1922-1943, lingering in German-occupied areas of the country until 1945.

The basic characteristic of fascism, in Italy and elsewhere, was its explosive mixture of passionate nationalism and revolutionary anti-Marxist Socialism. Fascists were unrelenting in their hatred of parliamentarianism and of communism. By parliamentarianism Fascists meant liberalism, democracy, freemasonry, everything advocating a system that would allow for divisions within the nation. Communism meant primarily Russian Bolshevism, but was expanded to include all variations of international socialism. Fascists were less clear in their positive attitudes.

In March 1919 a group of young war veterans, most of whom had been sympathetic to the anti-Marxist syndicalist brand of socialism, gathered in Milan around the former left-wing Socialist Benito Mussolini, who in 1914 had suddenly switched from pacifism to interventionism, and from internationalism to nationalism. For this he had been expelled from the Socialist party. In its anticapitalism, antiliberalism, and antimonarchism, the early Fascist program was still linked to Italian socialism. In its stress on the nation rather than the class as the foundation of society, emphasis on nationalism as the supreme social value, rejection of materialism as a conceptual framework, and acceptance of elitism, fascism denied socialism—as the term was then understood in Italy. When it came to power, fascism established political institutions derived from the recent experience of Leninist communism: the charismatic leader, the one-party state, the mass organization of the citizens, the subordination of all individual and collective aspects of life to an omnipotent ruler not responsible to any kind of popular assembly. From the Nationalist party (first an ally, later absorbed) fascism took its economic and social program; the institutions it advocated were derived from the recently reformulated Catholic corporatism.

Fascism was the most original contribution to be made by the Italian nation to human experience in recent times. It was also the most important since the Counter Reformation of the sixteenth century. Although later overshadowed by its German counterpart, which added racism to the composite ideology, Italian fascism set an example which, with variations, found many imitators. By 1939, when World War II started, more than half of the states in Europe had Fascist or semi-Fascist regimes with institutions largely patterned on Italian models. Two of them, Spain and Portugal, successfully weathered the storm of World War II. The military dictatorship in Japan (1932-1945), Brazilian *Integralismo* in the 1930's, Argentinian *Justicialismo* in the 1940's, Syrian Baathism and Egyptian Arab socialism in the 1950's received their inspiration from the Italian Fascist experience. As the result of World War II, most European Fascist movements lost power and disintegrated. The same happened to Japanese fascism. But fascism, usually going under different names, is far from dead. In nations ruled by revolutionaries who call themselves nationalists and socialists, there is fascism whenever the nationalist component prevails over the socialist. This is the case today in many authoritarian countries in the underdeveloped areas of the world.

A Minor Civil War

Not counting the Catholic party which, feeling its way carefully in the political arena, had its own goals, distrusted Liberals and Socialists equally, and as yet lacked the strength to aim at political power, there was, in the years immediately after World War I, a three-cornered contest in Italy between liberalism, socialism, and nationalism which facilitated the success of the Fascist movement. The Marxist majority of Italian Socialists were bent on destroying the Liberal state: on this count there was no difference between advocates of violence (the Communists after 1921) and democratic Marxists who rejected the use of violence and counted on universal suffrage to put them in power. Nationalists hated socialism in all its Marxist variations: in the success of the Socialists who stood for integral collectivism and for internationalism, they saw both the subversion of the social order and the end of the Italian nation as an independent, potentially influential factor in world affairs. At the same time they hated the Liberal state, on two main counts: its apparent inability to curb the Socialist threat, and its inability (actually unwillingness) to pursue an aggressive foreign policy.

The Nationalist party was small, but nationalism influenced the political behavior of a majority of educated Italians. It crossed class and party lines. Sincere, strong nationalistic feelings were shared by large sections not only of people who belonged to no party, but also of Liberals, democrats, Catholics, and non-Marxist Socialists. Nationalism therefore provided a common denominator for millions of Italians. In addition to the fear of a violent revolution like that taking place in Russia, in 1919-20 there were other events which exasperated the nationalistically inclined millions. The Versailles Peace Conference had opened in January 1919. The main topic of discussion was the peace treaty between the Western Allies (and Japan) and Germany, but the conference dealt with almost every problem related to the recently ended war. The dominant personality in the first few weeks was President Wilson, head of the American delegation. The document most frequently referred to was Wilson's Fourteen Points of January 1918. A kind of directorate, composed of the heads of the American, British, French, Italian, and Japanese delegations, guided the work of the conference. A thorny problem soon put the Italian delegation (Premier Orlando assisted by his foreign minister, Sonnino) in opposition to the others.

On October 30, 1918, when the Austro-Hungarian empire was disintegrating, the Italian majority of the citizens of Fiume (today Rijeka, a coastal city forty miles southeast of Trieste) had voted for annexation to Italy. The London agreement of April 1915 had not included Fiume among the Austro-Hungarian territories to be given to Italy. The city, with its hinterland inhabited entirely by Slavs, was claimed by Yugoslavia, the successor state formed late in 1918 by Serbia, Montenegro, and former Austro-Hungarian provinces inhabited by southern Slavs. Yugoslavia, like the other successor states, had the sympathies and could count on the support of the Americans, the British, and the French. Besides Fiume, Yugoslavia claimed Dalmatian and other districts granted to Italy by the London agreement, in which the majority of the population was Slavic. President Wilson made it clear to the Italians that they must either stand by the London agreement, and on the principle of legality have Dalmatia but not Fiume; or they must accept the principle of ethnic self-determination, in which case they could have Fiume but not Dalmatia.

In protest, on April 24, 1919, the Italian delegation abandoned the peace conference and returned to Italy. In its absence, the most important decisions concerning the peace treaty with Germany were taken. To the dismay of Italian nationalist public opinion, not a single former German colonial possession was assigned to Italy. The Italian delegation returned in time to sign the treaty, but the Fiume-Dalmatia question had not yet been settled. Because of the internal situation and the support the Allies had given to Yugoslavia, Premier Orlando resigned in June 1919; he was replaced by the progressive Liberal Nitti, supported by a coalition in which predominated groups that in 1914-15 had been against intervention. Nitti having announced that Italian troops would be withdrawn from Fiume pending an agreement between Italy and Yugoslavia, a band of war veterans composed mainly of Nationalists and revolutionary leftists (Republi-

cans and Syndicalists) and led by the patriot poet and war hero
D'Annunzio, took possession of Fiume and organized there the
Reggenza del Quarnaro. D'Annunzio established in the *Reggenza* a
corporate state which became a source of inspiration for Italian
Fascists (many of whom hoped, particularly in 1921 but also in 1922,
that D'Annunzio would become their leader).

Nitti's policy was anti-annexionist and anti-imperialist. The tense
internal situation prevented his government from solving external
problems: this task was taken over, successfully, by his successor
Giolitti, the old statesman who had been the main spokesman for
neutralism in 1914-15. His cabinet, formed in June 1920, included
the foremost Italian intellectual, Benedetto Croce, and the ablest
diplomat, Carlo Sforza. It was supported by a large, though not
cohesive, parliamentary majority. Paying no heed to Nationalist cries,
in August 1920 Sforza signed the treaty of Tirana which recognized
the independence of the small Balkan state of Albania. Italy kept
only a tiny island and a naval base. Troops that in the spring of 1919
had been landed in Ottoman Anatolia (part of which had been promised to Italy in the 1915 London agreement) were withdrawn in 1921-
22 as the result of an agreement in March 1921 between Italy and the
Turkish government. An accord with Greece recognized Greek rights
over islands in the Aegean sea, occupied by Italian forces in 1912
during the war between Italy and the Ottoman empire. The most
important of the agreements was the Treaty of Rapallo (November
1920), which fixed the boundaries between Yugoslavia and Italy.
Slavic areas of Istria and eastern Friuli, inhabited by about half a
million Croats and Slovenes, were kept by Italy in exchange for
renouncing Dalmatia (except for the city of Zara and a few small
islands inhabited mainly by Italians). Fiume became a free territory,
destined to serve as a sea outlet for northern Yugoslavia and land-
locked Danubian states. In December, Italian troops expelled from
Fiume D'Annunzio and his followers, who had refused to abide by
the treaty of Rapallo. A short-lived attempt at resistance caused
bloodshed in the *Reggenza* and deep resentment among Italian
patriots. Because of their anti-annexionist and anti-imperialist policies,
Nitti and Giolitti were branded as traitors by all rightist forces. The
Nationalists' hatred of the Liberal regime reached the intensity of
their obsessive hatred of socialism and communism.

On account of both their internal and external policies, Giolitti and his colleagues were abandoned by former supporters in and out of parliament. Resentful of a government which seemed to appease socialism and was frankly anti-annexionist, many moderates, without becoming Fascists themselves, swelled the ranks of those who admired, supported, and subsidized the Fascist movement. The Nationalist party could not hold its own against its more dynamic and better organized competitor. During the winter of 1921, groups of well-armed black-shirted Fascists, organized in "action squads," initiated a systematic terrorist campaign aimed at destroying Socialist and Communist political, economic, and cultural organizations. According to the Fascist interpretation, socialism and communism were the children of liberalism and democracy: therefore the ultimate goal of the Fascist campaign was the destruction of the Liberal democratic state. Liberals, freemasons, and progressive Catholics were assassinated by the Fascists together with Socialists and Communists. Socialists not inhibited by pacifism organized their own (usually rather modest) fighting groups, the *Arditi del Popolo*, and a small civil war began in many parts of northern and central Italy.

Hoping to strengthen his position in parliament, Giolitti called for new elections, held in May 1921. Socialists lost about a fifth of their seats, but fifteen Communists were elected to the House of Deputies. The Catholic vote increased. Thirty-seven Fascist deputies made their appearance next to the Nationalists. After the elections there was even less of a cohesive parliamentary majority than before. Any coalition depended on agreement between two of the three main political forces represented in parliament: Liberals, Socialists, and Catholics. Endless efforts to assemble a parliamentary majority were made in 1921-22. Responsible Liberal leaders were willing to come to terms with either Socialists or Catholics or both, but neither the Socialists (except for the few Socialdemocrats who had left the Socialist party in 1912, and the Reformists of 1922) nor the Catholics were willing to come to terms with the Liberals, who stood for private ownership of property and a secular state. Catholics following the lead of Sturzo wanted a coalition with the Socialists, but the Socialists' ideological materialism and practical secularism made an agreement impossible. The result of these divisions and antagonisms was a succession of minority cabinets with little authority.

While the government grew weaker and paralysis seemed to be leading to the disruption of the state, Fascists were becoming more and more active. Membership in action squads rose quickly from a few thousand to tens of thousands, to reach a total of several hundred thousand in the early autumn of 1922. To violence against individual opponents and systematic destruction of labor centers, cooperatives, and Socialist and Communist newspapers was now added the occupation of municipalities with leftist administrations. Armed Fascists, led by former army officers, would converge on a given village or town and eject mayors and aldermen; those who refused to leave were beaten and—if they resisted—killed. From small towns and villages, the Fascists progressed to provincial and even regional capitals like Bologna, Perugia, and Milan. At a meeting in Naples in October 1922, Mussolini, the *duce* of fascism, and his collaborators decided to deal with the government in Rome as they had dealt with municipal administrations.

Fascist squads numbering about thirty thousand men were concentrated in localities around the capital and from there, on October 28, they moved in on Rome. (The Fascist seizure of the capital was known as the *Marcia di Roma*, the march on Rome.) Not trusting the loyalty of the armed forces, whose officers were mostly sympathetic to fascism, the cabinet resigned. This left the king with the responsibility of deciding whether to give the government over to the Fascists or risk a civil war. After some hesitation he chose the first alternative, and on October 31 Mussolini formed his cabinet, with the collaboration of the Nationalists, the Catholics, and the right-wing Liberals. Several distinguished men belonging to no party were included in the cabinet.

In 1921-22 civilian and military authorities looked on Fascist activities with approval. They were convinced that in stamping out leftist subversion fascism was simply doing what the government ought to have done had it been able. Large segments of the public also looked on approvingly. It was a peculiarity of the Italian situation that Fascists (that is, sincere believers in Fascist ideology) were never numerous, but admirers and supporters of fascism (called *fiancheggiatori*) were many. Nationalists saw in the movement a chance to achieve national greatness. Property owners saw a means of eliminating the threat of collectivism. Catholics saw in fascism the instrument through which materialism, agnosticism, and atheism would be made to disappear from Italian life. Young progressive intellectuals, who identified Liberal democracy with conservatism and were impatient with seemingly slow democratic procedures, were sure that fascism provided a better answer to twentieth-century problems than the collectivism of the Socialists. After many years of turbulence, the establishment of a strong government headed by a young man (Mussolini was thirty-nine when he became prime minister) capable of enforcing order, ending strikes, eliminating inefficiency from the public services, and making its presence felt on the international scene caused millions of Italians to sigh with relief.

NINE

THE FASCIST DICTATORSHIP,

1922-1943

Fascism was Italy's radical right of the period immediately following World War I. The consent of large sections of the nation, just as much as its leaders' determination and the action squads' violence, helped it to seize power. Once in control, it moved rapidly toward totalitarianism. In Italy, fascism was more important for what it destroyed than for what it created. Identified for two decades with the nation and state, it left less of a trace than most had expected; in fact, fascism's highly praised achievements were found, afterwards, to have been mediocre.

The distinction between Fascists and the *fiancheggiatori*, the groups and forces that put them in power, was never obliterated. Fascists were rabid nationalists with a good dose of social radicalism, who prided themselves on their irrationality. There never were many of them. *Fiancheggiatori*, instead—conservatives of various hues fearful of subversive changes—were numerous. They included moderates who deserted their own Liberal regime; traditionalists bent on reasserting the authority of Catholicism; civilian and military officials and members of the business and land-owning communities clamoring for a strong government able to enforce authority and protect property rights; and millions of citizens who simply wanted order and discipline. The German alliance turned out to be the downfall of fascism. On evidence of Allied military superiority in World War II, the *fiancheggiatori* withdrew their support. Fascism collapsed, but the *fiancheggiatori* are still part of the Italian scene.

The Totalitarian State

Among the first measures that Mussolini's coalition government took were the replacement of parliamentary legislation with executive orders, the transformation of the action squads into a well-armed Fascist militia, and the establishment of censorship of the press. When the nation recovered from the initial shock of the Fascist *coup d'état* there was, briefly, an increase of opposition activities—not only by Socialists and Communists but also by Liberals, Democrats, and some Catholics. Opposition led to a recrudescence of Fascist violence. (The minor civil war fought before and after the Fascist seizure of power counted about four thousand dead, of whom three-fourths were anti-Fascists and one-fourth Fascists.) A mixture of blandishments and terrorism, as much as genuine approval of Fascist policies, helped the government to obtain a majority of votes at the general election in early 1924. The government candidates, including a number of distinguished politicians who came from Liberal, Catholic, and even Socialist ranks, received more than four million votes, to less than three million for the other parties.

In June 1924, the democratic Socialist leader Matteotti was murdered, and a severe crisis ensued. The opposition deputies left parliament and set up a loose coalition, called the *Aventino*. This, however, proved unable to shake Mussolini, who was supported by his militia, the enthusiastic devotion of party members, the king, the ecclesiastical hierarchy, millions of Italians whose first loyalty was to king or Church, the business community, and in general the conservative sections of the upper and middle classes. First the Communist, then the Catholic deputies left the anti-Fascist parliamentary coalition. Opposition collapsed. Attempts at agitation through street demonstrations failed to rouse the masses, and were quickly repressed.

Between January 1925 and November 1926 the Italian state was reorganized. Government power was concentrated in the hands of the *duce*, leader of fascism and head of the government, who was responsible only to the king and had a free hand in appointing his collaborators. The Grand Council of Fascism, composed of party leaders chosen by the *duce*, had vague functions but could, in a period of crisis, replace the head of government. Free elections were replaced by Soviet-style plebiscites, in which citizens could only vote "yes" for official candidates—a "no" vote meant anything from loss of job to imprisonment. Parliament was reduced to the role of consultative assembly. Local self-government was abolished. All communications media were brought under state control. Freedom of conscience for non-Catholics, always restricted in Italy, disappeared. What was left of freedom of the press, of teaching, of association, was abolished. New legal codes replaced the older ones, and the judiciary was deprived of its independence. The police force was expanded and its powers increased; also a secret political police was established. With the outlawing of all non-Fascist political organizations, the suppression of all non-Fascist publications, and the establishment of a Special Tribunal in November 1926 for crimes against the Fascist state, Italy became a totalitarian state.

In 1927 the Labor Chart fixed a few basic principles for reorganizing the economy along the lines of corporatism: strikes and lock-outs were banned; labor courts were set up to mediate between employers and employees; membership of employers and employees in government associations was made compulsory; a ministry of corporations was given wide authority on questions of prices, wages, profits, allocation of investments. In 1929 the Lateran Treaty ended the conflict between the Italian state and the Catholic Church caused by the annexation of the papal states in 1860-70, and created the independent Vatican state, which included the Vatican palace, St. Peter's, and a few other buildings. The papal blessing eliminated whatever doubts Catholics still had on the question of collaboration with fascism. The National Council of Corporations was also established in 1929: it was the Fascist counterpart of the Communist Gosplan which had been functioning for several years in the Soviet Union. In 1931 two government holding companies acquired controlling interests in all important Italian banks and in a number of large industrial enterprises. About a third of Italian industry was brought under direct or indirect government management. In 1938 racial laws were introduced to rid Italy of Jews and to separate any that remained from the rest of the Italian nation. There were then about sixty thousand Jews, a third of them refugees from racial persecution in central Europe. Also in 1938 the Fascist Grand Council abolished the House of Deputies and replaced it with an assembly composed of appointed members only.

On the surface, Fascist control of all aspects of Italian life was complete. But under the veneer of totalitarian uniformity there were divisions, and also some opposition. Obedience to the *duce* was an article of faith for Fascists, but this could not prevent the formation of quarreling cliques. Policies caused disagreements about which the public knew little or nothing. Mostly, however, politics took the form of palace intrigues in which personalities counted more than principles. The biggest bone of contention was the position of secretary-general of the Fascist party. On the question of the structure of the corporate economy there had been, in the early Thirties, sharp divisions between Fascists who came from antidemocratic revolutionary syndicalism (Rossoni, Bottai), and those who came from the reactionary authoritarian Nationalist party (Rocco, Federzoni). In the late Thirties there were pro-German Fascists (the *duce* himself, former party secretary Farinacci) and Fascists mistrustful of Germany (the best known being a former foreign minister, Grandi, later joined by his successor Ciano, Mussolini's son-in-law). From the Fascists distrustful of Germany came a revisionist group which spoke vaguely of a new, less totalitarian fascism, and opposed Mussolini in 1943 when Allied successes in North Africa and Sicily made it clear that the Allies would win the war.

The main non-Fascist organized forces supporting fascism in the Twenties were the civilian and military bureaucracy, the Catholic clergy, and the employers' associations. In spite of Fascist efforts to control them, each maintained its autonomy. Officials of the public administration were more Monarchist than Fascist, and the king could count on their loyalty. There was a rift in 1931 between fascism and the papacy on the question of the control of youth organizations. The papacy gave in, but the clergy kept their separate educational institutions. The death in 1939 of Pope Pius XI, always an enthusiastic admirer of fascism, weakened Fascist influence in the Vatican. Employers, especially the big business group, were weary of Fascist military adventures and did not share the Fascists' hatred of Western democracies.

Clandestine anti-Fascist activities had started in 1924 when the Communist party went underground. Its leaders, Gramsci and, after his arrest in 1926, Togliatti, owed their positions respectively to Zinoviev and Bukharin, the Comintern's chairmen. A democratic underground began to function in Florence in 1925. It was led by the historian Salvemini (later an exile, and Professor at Harvard in 1933-1948). In exile, Salvemini inspired the formation, in 1929, of the clandestine movement Justice and Liberty which, reorganized as the Action party in 1942, played a role in the anti-German Resistance of 1943-45. Most of its leaders in Italy were intellectuals, among them Parri, who became prime minister in 1945. Clandestine organizations of Constitutional Monarchists, freemasons, Socialists, and anarchists functioned briefly. As a result of the 1925-26 repression more than ten thousand anti-Fascists went into exile. A smaller number of racial refugees left Italy in the late Thirties. Among the distinguished intellectuals who chose exile and went to the United States were the conductor Toscanini and the scientist Fermi. About twenty thousand anti-Fascists were dealt with by the Special Tribunal. Far more numerous were those who were arrested and kept in prison or sent to internment camps without trial.

Achievements

Fascists prided themselves on their economic achievements, which they attributed to the superiority of corporatism over capitalism and collectivism, and to the policy of autarchy (national self-sufficiency), vigorously pursued since 1927. Agriculture was the main concern: energetic measures were adopted and vast sums were spent in increasing the yield of grains (particularly wheat), expanding industrial crops (sugar beet, tobacco, hemp, etc.), and improving livestock. Large marshy areas were reclaimed along the Tyrrhenian coast (Maremma north of Rome, and the Pontine marshes south of Rome) and in Sardinia. Several thousand farmers were settled in the North African colony of Libya, largely desertic, which had been occupied in 1911 and brought under effective Italian control in 1923-28. Railroads and roads were improved. Output of electricity was increased through the construction of a number of hydroelectric power plants. Chemical industries expanded. There is little doubt that Fascist leaders had a genuine conviction, shared by the public, that fascism had achieved miracles. Economists and statisticians wrote eulogies, while foreigners admired the new roads and the many new public buildings.

Although lack of discussion and criticism kept leaders and public alike ignorant of it, the real situation was quite different. The population grew by about a fifth from 1922-1942, but in spite of the large number of young people reaching working age every year, the labor force increased by only about 5 per cent; the result was that unemployment grew. During this period the gross national product, in 1964 dollars, went from about eleven billion to a little more than twelve billion, an increase smaller than that of the population; thus per capita income shrank. The decline in per capita income was gradual and small (5 to 6 per cent)—not enough to make an impact, or even bring awareness of what was going on, in a society where only praises of the regime were allowed. For people who had always been poor, like most Italians, a little more poverty made no difference. The agrarian policy gave small results in relation to the amount of capital invested; more of the scarce available capital had been absorbed by unproductive public expenses; autarchy had cut down imports, but fewer imports meant fewer exports; there was more wheat but less of other crops; and the main Italian industry, textiles, had declined considerably. Figures concerning the output of nationalized industries were falsified. Economically, the Fascists were living in a fool's paradise.

Military strength too was vastly overrated. A large and efficient military establishment being needed to implement an expansionist foreign policy, military expenses were increased and land, sea, and air forces were expanded. To these, and to a reinforced militarized police (*carabinieri*), were added the Fascist militia and five smaller Fascist corps. Military training was a main function of Fascist youth organizations. War and warlike spirit were lauded in speeches and in the press, while imposing parades stirred enthusiasm for the military forces. Italians were impressed.

Foreigners were likewise impressed: in the Thirties, the conviction that Italy was a strong military power was an important element on the international chessboard. Apparently, only German military experts doubted Italy's strength; the Nazi leaders, instead, shared the illusions of Italian Fascists and the views of most foreign observers. The difficulties the Italians met in the first four months of their war against Ethiopia (1935-36) should have been a warning, but in Italy and abroad these were attributed solely to the incompetence of an elderly commanding officer. World War II proved that numbers—which Italy had—count for little when organization is poor, weapons and training outdated, morale low, and generalship inept. When World War II started in 1939, however, Italy counted as a major military power, stronger in relation to the other great powers than in 1914.

The frankly imperialistic foreign policy of the Fascist regime had a single aim: territorial expansion. This included annexations, expansion of Italy's African colonial empire, and establishment of a sphere of influence. Italian nationalists (Fascists and non-Fascists alike) had always wanted the annexation of all areas claimable on ethnic, geographical, or historical grounds. After the post–World War I annexations of Trent and the South Tyrol, of Trieste and Julian Venetia, the nationalist program envisaged the annexation, sooner or later, of Corsica and Nice (belonging to France); Malta (then a British colony); the Ticino and smaller Swiss districts south of the Alpine divide; and Fiume and Dalmatia (belonging to Yugoslavia). It also envisaged the establishment of Italian protectorates over Albania in the Balkans and over Tunisia in North Africa (where about one hundred thousand Italians lived).

A vast colonial empire was claimed on the grounds that the fast-growing Italian nation needed living space, the Italian corporate and autarchic economy needed natural resources and an outlet for its industry, and national prestige and the role of a great power required an empire. Italian nationalists shared the then common illusion that colonies are a source of wealth; they were not aware that in recent times the acquisition of colonies had followed, not preceded, economic expansion. The Roman myth was an important element in stimulating imperialism. Northeastern Africa was the natural area for colonial expansion. Italian nationalists resented British presence in the Nile valley, French annexations in Somaliland and south of Libya, and the independence of Ethiopia, which had briefly been an Italian protectorate at the end of the nineteenth century. The Mediterranean, the Balkans, and the Middle East formed, according to the nationalists, Italy's natural sphere of influence. Ultimate goals were pretty clear.

Of the many passions that had given birth to fascism, hatred of the erstwhile World War I Allies was a major one. The Allies were accused of having deprived Italy of her legitimate fruits of victory. Animosity against the League of Nations was another article of faith in the Fascist creed: the League was supposed to be the instrument through which Great Britain and France planned to keep their ill-gotten gains. Because of this, victorious Italy felt she should champion the countries defeated in World War I, standing for the revision of the peace treaties which had dealt severely (unjustly, according to Fascists) with Germany, Austria, Hungary, and Bulgaria.

Fascist aims and claims found an immediate echo in the leaders of the near-Fascist regimes of Hungary and Bulgaria, and the clerical regime in Austria. The occupation of the Greek island of Corfu in September 1923 proved that Fascist imperialism was not purely verbal, and that the new Italian leaders were willing to pass from words to deeds. The murder of five Italian officers on the Albanian-Greek border was the pretext for this occupation. British and League pressure compelled Mussolini to order the withdrawal of Italian troops, but Greece had to pay a considerable indemnity. With the aim of calming Fascist territorial appetite, but with the result of stimulating it, the British agreed in 1924 to transfer to Italy a large area of East Africa west of the Juba river, inhabited mainly by Somalis; in 1925 they also agreed to transfer parts of western Egypt to Italy. Between 1926 and 1930 a rather loose bloc was formed by Italy through agreements with Albania, Hungary, Bulgaria, and Austria. It was the counterpart to the French-oriented Little Entente formed by Czechoslovakia, Rumania, and Yugoslavia. In the west Italy strengthened her relations with Spain, where the supporters of the De Rivera military dictatorship (1923-30) were admirers of Italian fascism.

The 1929-33 economic crisis was interpreted by Fascist leaders as the beginning of the end for capitalism, for Liberal democracy, and for the colonial empires of Western European nations—particularly the British and the French. In the early 1930's Mussolini and his collaborators decided to exploit the situation created by the economic crisis, the rapid rise of movements akin to fascism in Germany and Japan, and the growing sympathy for fascism in nations of all continents. Italian Fascist activity was particularly intense in the Middle East. Economic and cultural exchanges had definite political aims. At various levels (official and nonofficial, open and clandestine) contacts were established with the Egyptian Green Shirts, anti-British and anti-Jewish leaders of Palestinian Moslems, and the Syrian and Iraqi extreme nationalists (who later founded the National Socialist Baath movement); also, further west, with the Algerian League of Ulemas and the Tunisian neo-Destour.

The chief immediate goal of Fascist expansionism, however, was Ethiopia, then one of four independent African states and one still governed by its traditional ruler. In 1933-34 roads and fortifications were built in the two Italian colonies of Eritrea and Somalia bordering on Ethiopia, military depots were established, garrisons strengthened, dissatisfied Ethiopian notables bribed. On December 5, 1934, Italian troops fought Ethiopians at Walwal, in an area disputed between Ethiopia and Italian Somalia. Because the Fascists were determined to wage war, efforts at mediation made by the League of Nations gave no results. British and French mediation efforts (through the Hoare-Laval proposals, highly favorable to Italy) failed for the same reason, as did attempts to arbitrate through the International Court of Justice. On October 3, 1935, Italian troops invaded Ethiopia. When Marshal Badoglio replaced the incompetent General De Bono as commander of the invading forces, the Italians advanced rapidly. On May 5, 1936, Addis Ababa was occupied; four days later the country was annexed by Italy, to whose king Mussolini gave the title of emperor of Ethiopia. The economic sanctions the League tried to apply against Italy only showed that economic pressure is not enough to prevent wars. In December 1937 Italy withdrew from the League.

The German Shadow

Central European events of 1932-36 proved more important than the activities of Italian Fascists in the Middle East and East Africa. The formation of a National Socialist government in Germany under Adolf Hitler, in January 30, 1933, had been hailed with enthusiasm by Italian Fascists. National socialism and fascism shared similar ideologies, advocated similar institutions, had similar goals. The main difference was that the National Socialist concept of nation was more racial than the Fascist. This accounts for the anti-Semitism in national socialism, and its absence in fascism (many Italian Jewish business people and intellectuals had been enthusiastic supporters of fascism). The difference disappeared when anti-Semitic legislation was introduced in Italy.

There was one bone of contention between Hitler's Germany and Mussolini's Italy: the control of Austria, where in 1933 a clerical dictatorship had abolished the parliamentary democratic regime. For Germans, Austria was German and therefore should be part of the German state. For Italians, Austria was an indispensable buffer state and should remain independent. The murder of the Austrian dictator Dollfuss in 1934 by National Socialists caused friction between Italy and Germany. The problem was solved in 1936 when, in exchange for the support Germany had given to Italy during the Ethiopian war, Mussolini decided to let Austria go. With the agreement of October 26, 1936, was born what became known as the Rome-Berlin Axis. Strengthened in November 1937 by Italy's joining the Anti-Comintern (anti-Communist) Pact between Germany and Japan of the previous year, it led to the formal alliance of May 22, 1939 between Italy and Germany (the Steel Pact).

In the late Thirties, German influence rapidly superseded Italian in the Danubian and Balkan revisionist states and in those where, through internal or external pressure, Fascist and near-Fascist regimes were established. In March 1938 German troops invaded Austria, which was annexed to the German Reich. As the result of the Munich agreement of September 28, 1938, with which the British and French governments—desperately trying to avoid a war—gave in to all German demands, Germany annexed about a fifth of Czechoslovakia in October. Taking advantage of the agitation of Slovak nationalists against the Czechs, German troops occupied the Czech capital in March 1939 and a German protectorate was established over the non-Slovak areas of the former Czecho-Slovak state. Agreements with Hungary in February 1939, and with Rumania in April of the same year, further strengthened the German position. Only Albania, occupied and annexed in April 1939, remained to Italy, whose king added to his many titles that of king of this little Balkan state.

Fascist influence was spreading. On July 17, 1936, Spanish generals who had for some time been in touch with Italian Fascist agents started a military uprising against the republican regime established in Spain in April 1931. Behind the uprising was a coalition of Fascists, traditionalists, nationalists, and clericals who represented influential groups and classes (landowners, the clergy, the military), and counted on the support of the devout Catholic masses of the population. The revolt was successful in the western half of Spain. It failed in the areas where a majority of the working classes, influenced since the nineteenth century by Russian anarcho-syndicalism, later also by democratic socialism and more recently on a small scale by communism, had turned against clerical traditionalism. There followed a tragic civil war which lasted until March 1939 and in which about a million people were killed. Fearful of an expansion of hostilities, the British and French governments arranged and respected an international agreement against intervention. Italy signed the agreement but sent considerable aid to the nationalist regime formed by the rebel generals; the Italian contribution included about one hundred thousand "volunteers." In April 1939 the government formed in Spain by the victorious rightist coalition joined the Anti-Comintern Pact.

By 1939 Italy had lost all autonomy in external affairs—partly because of the overwhelming strength of the German ally, partly because Mussolini and his clique were convinced that Italy and Germany should remain strictly united on the grounds that fascism was going to be victorious everywhere and Italy would share in the general triumph. But Italian and German leaders underestimated their opponents' strength. Apparently it had been understood at the time of the signing of the Steel Pact that, even should a war prove indispensable for the realization of ultimate National Socialist and Fascist goals, Germany would not wage war until 1942. That the invasion of Poland would start World War II was not expected: why would Great Britain and France fight for Poland if they had not fought for Czechoslovakia? The Soviet Union had agreed to a partition of Poland, with the pact of August 23, 1939. In the United States, isolationism neutralized the efforts made by President Roosevelt, a foe of fascism and national socialism. Nationalistic agitation was weakening the British Commonwealth and Empire. Japan was in firm control of the northeastern and eastern Chinese provinces. In short, prospects for fascism seemed excellent.

Great Britain and France declared war on Germany on September 3. Mussolini was taken aback. The Ethiopian war (and ensuing difficult "pacification"), and intervention in Spain and the Balkans, had depleted military depots and caused considerable disruption in the none too efficient military organization. As it was not certain that the Allied declaration of war would be followed by hostilities, and Hitler was apparently not keen on Germany's ally joining the fray at that time, Mussolini decided to wait. In Berlin there was impatience: Germany again took the military initiative, invading Denmark and Norway in April 1940, and the Netherlands, Luxembourg, Belgium, and France in the next month. Success followed on success. Not to be left out by the German ally, Mussolini declared war against Great Britain and France on June 10 (and after the Japanese attack on Pearl Harbor, against the United States on December 11, 1941). There had been little or no fighting between French and Italians when France surrendered on June 22, 1940. Germany and Japan went from victory to victory until August 1942. But not Italy. What Italian territorial expansion there was, mostly at the expense of Yugoslavia, was a German gift.

One month after the signing, on September 27, 1940, of the German-Italian-Japanese pact for a ten-year military and economic alliance, Italian troops stationed in Albania invaded Greece. There they met with a total lack of success and Germany had to rescue her Italian ally, attacking Greece through Yugoslavia in April 1941. The German campaign in the Balkans was only a sideline, but it upset the German timetable. It delayed the attack against the Soviet Union until June 22, 1941, and was a major factor in preventing the Germans from capturing Moscow and Leningrad before winter set in.

The Italian invasion of Egypt from Libya in September 1940 was topped by a successful British counteroffensive in December. In the spring of 1941 German troops under General Rommel came to the rescue of the Italians in North Africa. From then on the Germans had the chief responsibility in North African fighting. In January 1941 a small British force of about thirty thousand men attacked Italian East Africa, garrisoned by several hundred thousand men. The British, received favorably by the population, met with unexpected success, and by June Italian resistance had collapsed. The Ethiopian ruler, an exile in London since 1936, returned to Addis Ababa. Italian raids against British bases in Malta and Gibraltar failed. In naval encounters in the Mediterranean the British defeated superior Italian forces.

At first the Italian public heard little about these reverses, but then news began to filter through. As already mentioned, the foundation of the Italian Fascist regime had been not so much the Fascist movement itself, which was relatively small, but the support given to it by non-Fascist admirers; that support now began to weaken. Then came the turn of the military tide with the British stand at El Alamein in June 1942, the American stand at Guadalcanal in August 1942, and the Soviet stand at Stalingrad in September 1942. The summer stand was followed by British, American, and Soviet offensives in the autumn—in North Africa, the Pacific, and Russia. In May 1943 German-Italian forces in North Africa surrendered to the Anglo-American allies commanded by General Eisenhower. In June, Allied forces took the island of Pantelleria, between Tunisia and Sicily. The Italian garrison put up no resistance. On July 10, British and American troops landed in Sicily, where the well-equipped Italian divisions, consisting of several hundred thousand men, melted away. Small German forces fought a vigorous delaying action until August 18, when they completed the evacuation of the island.

ITALY IN 1965

TEN

EXPERIMENT IN DEMOCRACY

Military defeats and foreign invasions, with the extensive suffering and destruction they caused, brought chaos to Italy in 1943-45. During this time of chaos forces operating within the nation were reorganized and redistributed. The changes amounted to a transformation, one which is still taking place. Much remained of the political, intellectual, and economic heritage of the recent and remote past. To this was added a great deal that was new.

Democracy was the political formula offered to the Italian nation by the groups that had been active in the war-time Resistance. There was little enthusiasm for the formula, but most people accepted it. Many agreed that it was the only compromise guaranteeing peaceful coexistence in a differentiated society, and a few thought it might stimulate progress. In a modernized version, political Catholicism again occupied the center of the national stage. Its influence was held in check mainly by a moderate form of Communism. The fiction of Italy's being a great power was abandoned, and war-mongering ceased. In international affairs Italy aimed at agreements and the avoidance of conflicts.

The emancipating effect of the war-time disruption was evident in a new-found intellectual vigor which in the period after the war raised Italian achievements in literature and other fields to high levels. Illiteracy ceased to be a major problem. By 1964 the prewar gross national product had multiplied three and a half times. This was achieved in a system that integrated private and public initiative.

Although during the postwar period Italy has been remarkably steady in spite of the transformation taking place, there have been elements of instability and unrest; these make forecasts difficult even for the immediate future.

The Resistance

The Allied invasion of Sicily in the summer of 1943 spelled the end of fascism. Partly because of Mussolini's illness at the end of 1942, his dictatorship had become inefficient. Consequently there was a freedom which, however limited, Italians had not known since the early 1920's. Politically active Italians included the minority of convinced Fascists, the smaller clandestine anti-Fascist minority, and the larger, rather loose-knit groups of *fiancheggiatori*. Peace was the main concern of most of the Italians who were not politically motivated. This was hardly surprising considering that, counting minor and major conflicts, Italy had been involved in wars since December 1934.

No popular uprising resulted from mounting military defeats, but two separate conspiracies had been making headway in Rome. A Fascist clique led by Grandi, Ciano, Bottai, Federzoni, De Bono, and others hoped that the removal of Mussolini and his pro-German close collaborators would enable Italy to come to terms with the Allies while preserving a slightly modified Fascist regime. Among the *fiancheggiatori*, influential monarchists led by Duke Acquarone and Marshal Badoglio wanted to replace fascism with a royal dictatorship. They were certain that, internally, such a dictatorship would be able to count on the support of all other *fiancheggiatori*, especially the Catholic Church, property owners, and military and civilian bureaucracies; and externally it could more easily than the Fascists approach the Allies and get Italy out of the war.

An Allied air raid on Rome on July 19, 1943, and the news that Hitler, at a meeting in Feltre, had refused the aid requested by Mussolini, forced the hands of the two sets of conspirators. At a meeting of the Grand Council of Fascism on July 24, Mussolini's proposal to continue the war on Germany's side was opposed by the Fascist conspirators, who obtained a majority of twenty to seven (there was one abstention). This however was not enough to bring about a political change. The members of the Grand Council did not have control over the armed forces; the *duce* was still in the saddle. All he had to do was to put his opponents in jail. On the twenty-fifth, the monarchist conspirators, informed of what had happened in the Grand Council, persuaded the king to order Mussolini's arrest. This took place after a friendly interview in the afternoon between the head of state and the head of government. On the advice of the monarchist conspirators the king appointed Marshal Badoglio head of the government; it was a *coup d'état*, not a revolution. Within hours of the radio announcement that Badoglio was in charge, all Fascist organizations melted away; this was a revolution—a bloodless one. The Fascists went into hiding. A few fled to Germany. Although some experts had long maintained that fascism was just a veneer covering the Italian nation, hardly anyone had realized how very thin the veneer was.

The new government was faced with a difficult and dangerous position, both internally and externally. Structurally authoritarian, it could not enforce its authority. It had no organized political support capable of mobilizing monarchism, Catholicism, and business and overcoming the general war-weariness. It was hated by anti-Fascists as much as by Fascists. Although the clandestine Action and Communist parties were illegal, they began to act openly. In many parts of Italy the Socialist party, the Christian Democratic party (a revised version of the 1919 Popular party), the Liberal party, and others were quickly reorganized. Actionists, Socialists, and Communists formed anti-Fascist committees, sometimes joined by Catholics and Liberals. After the armistice these committees, the Committees of National Liberation (CLN's), gave stimulus and unity to the anti-German insurgence known as the Resistance.

At the end of July 1943 the Germans had seven divisions in Italy, while the Allies were fighting in Sicily and were preparing to land on the mainland soon. The Badoglio government sent agents to the Allies while telling the Germans that Italy would continue to fight on Germany's side. Immediately after the *coup d'état* the Germans occupied the Alpine passes. While making plans for occupying the whole country, they increased the number of divisions there to seventeen. Contacts with the Allies established early in August led to secret negotiations and to the signing of an armistice at Cassabile in Sicily on September 3. On that day the British, under General Montgomery, landed at Reggio on the mainland. The armistice was made public in the evening of September 8, when a large American and British expeditionary force under General Clark was approaching the beaches of Salerno, not far from Naples.

As fascism had unexpectedly disintegrated within hours of the July 25 *coup d'état*, so the Italian state disintegrated following the announcement of the armistice. The occupation of the north and center by the Germans and the south by the Allies was only part of the picture. Fearing arrest by the Germans, the king, Marshal Badoglio, and most ministers fled Rome. Officials in responsible positions went into hiding. Public services stopped functioning. Worst of all was the sudden collapse of the army, which then consisted of more than eighty divisions. Most soldiers and officers deserted; sporadic resistance was offered to the Germans but was soon overcome. The only armed forces to stay intact were the *carabinieri*, who did their best to help and protect the population, and the navy, which joined the Allies.

Nearly twenty months of atrocious warfare followed. Two wars were being fought simultaneously in Italy: one between the Allies and the Germans (each having Italian auxiliaries), the other between Italian patriots and anti-Fascists on one side, Germans and Fascists on the other. After a delaying action at Salerno the Germans slowly retreated to a fortified line north of Naples, reached by the Allies between October 1943 and early January 1944. An Allied landing at Anzio (January 1944) failed to dislodge the Germans. But success crowned the Allied attack on Cassino in May, which led to the liberation of Rome (June 4) and compelled the Germans to withdraw to another fortified line north of Florence, held until April 1945. The Allied offensive began on April 5 (when Germany had already been invaded both from the east and the west). The German surrender was signed on April 29 and fighting stopped on May 2. About thirty thousand British and twenty thousand Americans died in the Italian campaign. Strategically, the 1943 invasion of Sicily and the Allied landing at Salerno leading to the occupation of the important airfields of Foggia was a necessity. On the other hand, opinions are divided on the military and political usefulness of the 1944 and 1945 campaigns in Italy.

The Badoglio government, reorganized in Allied territory, declared war on Germany on October 13, 1943. Rescued by the Germans, Mussolini proclaimed, under their protection, a republic (the Italian

Social Republic) and organized a Fascist government. But in September insurgent activities had already begun in most of German-held Italy, and they soon developed into a large-scale Partisan (Resistance) movement. A minority of the Partisans were loyal to the king; most owed their allegiance to the Committees of National Liberation. In Allied-occupied Italy the CLN became the government in June 1944 when Marshal Badoglio resigned, the king transferred his powers to his son the crown prince (briefly king for a few days in 1946 as Humbert II), and a pre-Fascist premier, Bonomi (chairman of the Rome CLN in the period of German occupation), became prime minister again.

In German-occupied Italy the clandestine CLN's, composed of Actionists (republican democrats), Christian Democrats (Catholics), Communists, Liberals, and Socialists gave cohesion and unity to the Partisan movement, acting as an underground anti-Fascist government. With German aid, forces of Mussolini's Fascist republic tried to repress the Partisans, but failed. This civil war was particularly intense in Florence in August 1944 and in Turin in April 1945. The Partisan insurgency helped the Allies considerably, and raised Italian morale. During the last days of the insurgency Mussolini was killed, while trying to escape to Switzerland. The two wars and German massacres of civilians and prisoners caused heavy human losses between September 1943 and May 1945: on the Resistance side alone, more than one hundred thousand people died. Between a quarter and a third of the nation's wealth had been destroyed. Real wages in 1945 were only 26 per cent of what they had been in 1941. American aid, governmental and private, checked famine.

The Italian Republic

The range, the violence, the suddenness of the 1943-45 events, and the active participation of millions of Italians in the Resistance, helped to widen the break with the recent Fascist past. *Coup d'état* and revolution, the sufferings of international war and civil war, family disruptions and famine, had created new emotions and passions that obliterated the previous ones. From the crisis came change. Fascism was gone. As an idea it lingered in a small minority (not more than one in twenty adult Italians, according to electoral returns from 1946 to 1964), nostalgic for the dreams on which the nation had been fed for twenty years. The spokesmen for what had been the dominant forces in pre-Fascist Italy, the Liberals and secular non-collectivist democrats, returned to the fore briefly, but few followed them. The intellectual, political, and economic revolt against liberalism once identified with the Socialist movement had gained ground, but its impact was weakened by the deep cleavage between a socialist and a communist party. Political Catholicism, the nineteenth century opponent of liberalism defeated in 1859-70, was now—as represented by the Christian Democratic party—the dominant force in Italy.

The remarkable political feature of postwar Italy was the establishment and survival of free democratic institutions. Although there were comparatively few democrats in Italy, the state was organized along democratic lines and it functioned. The presence of Allied (British and American) troops was an important factor in the establishment of democratic institutions. The main factors making for their survival were the balance existing between political Catholicism and Marxism, the basic moderation of most Italians (even when members of extreme parties), and the sense of responsibility felt by most leading politicians.

A coalition of the parties forming the war-time CLN governed Italy until free elections in June 1946 made clear the will of Italian citizens. Bonomi resigned the premiership in June 1945, and the Central Committee of National Liberation designated Parri, Action party leader and distinguished Resistance figure, as prime minister. A consultative assembly of appointed members in which each CLN party had equal representation was organized. The right-wing parties of the CLN (Christian Democratic and Liberal parties) compelled Parri to resign in December 1945. He was succeeded by the Christian Democrat leader De Gasperi, who had been the last secretary-general of the pre-Fascist Popular party. A clerk in the Vatican library, he had never renounced the democratic convictions of his youth.

On June 2, 1946, a referendum was held: out of a total vote of over twenty-two million, twelve million Italians voted for a republican form of government. King Humbert II went into exile. Results of the elections for a constituent assembly held the same day shattered the fiction that the CLN parties had equal strength. The Christian Democrats polled over 35 per cent of the vote (a percentage corresponding approximately to that of practicing and nonpracticing

Catholics). The Marxists were divided about equally between Socialists and Communists (approximately 21 per cent and 19 per cent respectively of the total vote). Liberals and democrats, opposed to both political Catholicism and collectivism, received about 16 per cent of the vote. The balance went to a number of smaller groups.

For a few months after the elections De Gasperi headed a tripartite coalition of Catholics, Socialists, and Communists. The Communists used their position to obstruct governmental activity, trying to demonstrate to Italians that Western-type liberal democracy could not work, and should be replaced by Soviet-type dictatorial people's democracy. Socialists acrimoniously debated the problem of their collaboration with the Communists, and on that problem the anti-Communist minority, led by Saragat, seceded and formed a separate Social Democratic party. In May 1947 the tripartite coalition collapsed. For twelve years Italy was governed by a parliamentary coalition of Catholics, Social Democrats, and two smaller parties, the Liberal party and the Republican party, the one heir to once-dominant pre-Fascist monarchical liberalism, the other to pre-Fascist republican democracy. This was called a center coalition. Cabinets were always headed by a Christian Democrat, and at times included all members of the parliamentary coalition, at others only Christian Democrats and independents.

In the Italian constitutional system prime ministers need to be backed by a parliamentary majority: this the Catholic leaders usually had. De Gasperi (who died in 1954) was prime minister until August 1953. Succeeding prime ministers, according to which group predominated in the Christian Democratic party, were spokesmen for the right wing (Pella, Scelba, Tambroni), for the center (Segni, Zoli, Leone), for the left wing (Fanfani, Moro). Animated debates accompanied each cabinet change. However, government policies remained essentially the same: support of new dealism (in American terms) in internal economic and social affairs, pro-Americanism and advocacy of European unity in external affairs.

The republican constitution had been approved by the constituent assembly in 1947. Owing largely to the balance between the two main Italian postwar forces, political Catholicism and Communism (then supported by a majority of the Socialist party), the constitution was essentially democratic. New elections were held in April 1948. The tense atmosphere in Italy reflected the cold war between the Soviet Union and the United States which was growing in intensity, and the widening gulf between Eastern and Western Europe.

Italian Americans participated in the elections through a massive campaign of letters sent to Italian relatives and friends asking them to vote for anti-Communist parties, i.e. for the Catholics and their allies. The united front of Communists and Socialists polled fewer votes than expected: 31 per cent of the total vote (the balance of the Socialist vote, another 7 per cent, went to the new Social Democratic party). With 48.5 per cent of the vote, the Christian Democrats elected a majority of deputies and senators. Altogether the parliamentary center coalition had 62 per cent of the vote. Parliament elected president of the republic the distinguished economist and former minister of finance Einaudi (1948-55) who, like his predecessor the provisional president De Nicola, had been in pre-Fascist days an active Liberal monarchist. By the elections of 1953 fear of communism had abated, and the Christian Democratic party polled a more realistic 40 per cent and its allies 9 per cent. They still nevertheless had a slight majority in parliament. Communists (23 per cent of the vote) and Socialists (13 per cent) were still cooperating, but presented separate candidates. The Christian Democrat Gronchi was elected President of the Republic in 1955 (to be succeeded in 1962 by Segni, another leader of the same party).

In 1960 the clerical right wing of the Christian Democratic party tried to govern the country through a rightist coalition, supported by a parliamentary majority which included monarchists and neo-Fascists. Demonstrations organized by all parties left of center, from the moderate Republicans to the Communists, compelled the rightist cabinet to resign. Since then the party has been controlled by an uneasy coalition between center and left wing.

Meanwhile the 1956 events in the Communist world (denunciation of Stalin, agitation in Poland, revolution in Hungary) had caused a crisis among Socialists, who gradually drifted away from the Communists. Through the intermediary of the Social Democratic leader Saragat, Christian Democrats and Socialists were induced to collaborate. In 1961, Socialists were supporting the Christian Democrats in parliament, and finally, in 1963, what in 1919-1922 had been the main aspiration of the founders of the Catholic Popular party was realized:

the coalition of Catholics and Socialists, united (at least theoretically) in their opposition to free enterprise advocated by Italian Liberals, and to dictatorship advocated by Communists and neo-Fascists.

The Catholic-Socialist coalition was based (again, theoretically) on Catholic concessions to the Socialists in the economic and social fields, on Socialist concessions to the Catholics in education, state-Church relationships, and control of communications media. The pro-Communist wing of the Socialist party seceded and early in 1964 formed a new party. At the 1964 local elections the Communist vote was 26 per cent. Adding fellow-traveling votes, the Communist electoral strength was about the same as it had been in 1948—index of remarkable stability. The Catholic-Socialist-Socialdemocratic-Republican coalition formed in 1963 and reorganized in 1964 had 56.5 per cent of the total vote, a little less than the Catholic-led coalition of 1948—again an index of remarkable stability.

Foreign Relations

Consistency characterized the foreign policy of the Italian republic, particularly after the Communists were eased from the government in May 1947. In February of that year the independent Sforza was appointed minister of foreign affairs, the position he had held in the cabinet of the Liberal Giolitti in 1920-21. European and Atlantic Western solidarity and the United Nations had no more sincere supporters than Sforza and De Gasperi, who gave Sforza his full backing. Sforza was a convinced and dedicated spokesman for democracy as it had developed in the North Atlantic areas. Close collaboration with the United States (where he had spent several years as an exile) and with European democracies was the keynote of his policy and that of his successors, down to the Social Democratic leader Saragat, foreign minister in the Catholic-Socialist coalition of 1963-65.

The peace treaty between Italy and the Allies was signed on February 10, 1947. It was the result of laborious and tense negotiations between American, British, French, and Soviet diplomats. The large territorial acquisitions made during the first phase of World War II were of course lost. Italy also had to renounce districts on her northeast border, covering about 3,000 square miles, where Yugoslavs predominated; four small areas in the western Alps; and all her overseas dependencies. Libya, first administered by the British, soon became an independent kingdom. Eritrea was federated with Ethiopia. The Aegean islands were transferred to Greece. Somalia, destined to become independent, was administered by Italy as a United Nations trusteeship until 1960. Albania was once again independent. Reparations to be paid chiefly to Ethiopia, Greece, and Yugoslavia amounted to two hundred and sixty million dollars. The Italian army was reduced to 250,000 men, the air force to 350 planes, the navy to fewer than 40 vessels. Sforza was able to obtain first a revision of several economic clauses of the treaty and later the abolition of the military clauses. The Italian public's relative indifference to the peace terms showed that nationalism had weakened considerably.

Most painful of all for Italians was the proposed loss of Trieste, claimed by the Yugoslav Communist regime then actively supported by the Soviet Union. To prevent Yugoslav annexation, the Western Allies obtained from the Soviet Union that the city and a small surrounding area should become a free territory, administered partly by them and partly by Yugoslavia. In March 1948 Sforza persuaded the American, British, and French governments to issue a declaration recognizing the city's right to rejoin the mother country at some future date. The quarrel of Yugoslavia's dictator Tito with Stalin (June 1948) helped the Italian position. As a result of a British-American agreement of October 1953, Trieste and the area of the free territory north of the city were returned to Italy in 1954. Yugoslavia formally annexed the area south of the city that had been under her administration.

As mentioned in Chapter One, in spite of the opposition of Communists and fellow-travelers and recurring waves of neutralism, Italy has participated actively in most of the initiatives aiming at the establishment of common institutions tying Western countries to each other. An attempted customs union with France failed because of the combined nationalist and Communist opposition in the two countries. A few days after the speech of the American secretary of state, General Marshall, at Harvard on June 5, 1947, the Italian government asked that the question of European economic recovery through American aid (the Marshall Plan) be discussed not only by the Big Three, as the British and French had suggested, but by all European states concerned. The Marshall Plan was the first major step in the European and North Atlantic cooperative efforts that, it is hoped, will lead to the creation of a community of nations linked by economic, political, and military ties. Italy was a charter member of the Organization for European Economic Cooperation, the Council of Europe, the North Atlantic Treaty Organization, the Coal and Steel Community, the European Common Market. Italian government circles were saddened by the failure to set up a European Defence Community in 1954. United States proposals in the early 1960's for creating a multilateral nuclear force were accepted more readily by Italy than by other American allies. Growing neutralism did not adversely affect the desire of parliamentary majorities to see a strengthening of European and North Atlantic organizations.

Italy's membership in the United Nations was repeatedly vetoed by the Soviet Union, although she had been allowed to join all the major specialized UN agencies, including UNESCO, the World Health Organization, the International Labor Office, and the Food and Agriculture Organization (which has had headquarters in Rome since 1951). One of the agreements included in the package deal between the United States and the Soviet Union during the first international thaw after Stalin's death was the admittance of Italy into the United Nations in 1955. Without expressing reservations about the American position, Italy sided with the United States in all major crises of the 1947-1964 period.

Italy's relations have also been particularly friendly with the German Federal Republic and Great Britain. Political and economic affinity favored close ties with the Federal Republic: in both countries political Catholicism was the dominant force, government majorities supported a consistently pro-American policy in foreign affairs, and free enterprise played a major role in economic expansion. Moreover, the Federal Republic has been an important outlet for Italian surplus labor and Italian agricultural products. In Great Britain Italian governments saw, especially after De Gaulle's return to power in France in 1958, the country that could best balance the strengthened French state. Efforts were made to establish close economic and cultural relations with newly independent states in the Middle East and Africa. In the early 1960's the activities, among the fewer than two hundred thousand German-speaking inhabitants of the Alto Adige (or South Tyrol), of an Austrian-based nationalist and terrorist movement caused difficulties between Italy and Austria.

All in all, the Italian republic played on the international scene the role of a peaceful, second-rate power whose main interest was to lessen antagonism and tension.

The Nation's Achievements

As often happens in societies where there is freedom of expression, party politics and the seamy side of public and private life (intrigues, corruption, immorality) stole the limelight in postwar Italy. In reality politics, though important, represented only a part, not even a large one, of national life, and corruption and immorality concerned only small sectors of the nation. There were solid achievements at both public and private levels. At the public level democratic institutions functioned, civil liberties were guaranteed, order was maintained, extremist movements became less extreme. Political, economic, and social stability was the main preoccupation of the center, right-of-center, and left-of-center coalitions governing the country after the Communists were eased out of the government in 1947. On the private level intellectual life was lively; efficient and imaginative hard work contributed to the remarkable expansion of the economy; standards of living improved; far-reaching changes modified personal relationships at the family and the class level. Public and private achievements reflected the moderately progressive aspirations of a majority of the citizens. There were shadows on the Italian scene, but they never darkened the whole picture.

Public administration had become inefficient and cumbersome under the Fascist regime; now it was greatly improved. Local self-government—the foundation of the democratic process—was extended, and cautious steps were taken toward regional autonomy. The judiciary gained its independence and a constitutional court was created, partly patterned on the United States Supreme Court. In the field of education, illiteracy practically disappeared among the younger people, and secondary as well as elementary public education became a right instead of a privilege. Higher education expanded, gradually opening to all who qualified for it. Public libraries increased and scientific research was stimulated. Legal discrimination between the sexes was lessened.

The remarkable stability of wholesale prices between 1947 and 1961 (there was a variation of less than 4 per cent) and of the Italian currency on the international market resulted from sound management of public finance, and created an environment that enabled the real gross national product to reach, in 1964, a level more than three times higher than before the war. Postwar economic expansion sharply contrasted with the stagnation of the Fascist period. Unemployment and underemployment, chronic scourges, were greatly diminished, and material life was being transformed everywhere, in the underdeveloped south perhaps more than anywhere else. Social security was improved and provided most of the population with an economic security unprecedented in Italy.

Public enterprises (including state-owned industries with nearly three hundred thousand employees) and publicly subsidized investments stimulated economic growth without restricting private enterprise. Actually the private sector of the economy expanded more than the public sector. The intelligent use of public initiative included a series of far-reaching measures. For example, in 1950 the *Cassa del Mezzogiorno* was created; this is a fund which in fourteen years has invested the equivalent of about four billion dollars in the underdeveloped south. A state oil monopoly established under the Fascist regime was transformed into a public authority competing with private enterprise; it soon became one of the largest Italian corporations. In 1962, enterprises producing electric power were consolidated into a public authority, and more electricity was produced at a lower cost. According to a plan approved by parliament in 1964, government loans at a low rate of interest aimed at facilitating the transformation of land tenure and at stimulating the mechanization of agriculture. The 1964 recession marked a pause in a process of fast expansion. In spite of it, the Italian GNP increased about 4 per cent in 1964.

Many of the changes characterizing the first two decades of postwar Italy were due to government action. Even more were due to the initiative of private citizens. Achievements at the level of private activities were remarkable, especially when compared to the slow pace of change and progress and long periods of stagnation known by previous generations. A transformation in the Italian way of life, which had been expected after unification but had not materialized, which had begun rather slowly before World War I and had then been interrupted by the war and by Fascist totalitarianism, was now taking place. No one of course could say how far or how deep the transformation would go.

The downfall of fascism meant the freeing of intellectual energies, the primary source of progress. Official and unofficial censorship disappeared, and this made possible the weakening of the heavy crust of conformity and provincialism. Theoretically the two largest and most influential groups of educated Italians, the Catholics and the Marxists, each aimed at establishing its monopoly over the activities of the mind; but, although in the name of traditional morality the Catholic clergy advocated censorship, there was no monopoly and little censorship. Intellectual liberty did exist, and it was giving good results.

A large crop of able young writers appeared on the literary scene: novelists, poets, critics. There was only one Nobel Prize winner, The poet Quasimodo, but many were on his level. Publishing houses became dynamic. The reading public expanded considerably. Scores of magazines of opinion provided a badly needed forum for discussing new ideas. Artists left the conventional and the traditional and sought new ways to express themselves. Italian culture no longer vegetated in isolation. Writers and artists won acclaim abroad, and to their great advantage Italians became better acquainted with the intellectual scene in other countries. American fiction was particularly admired. Translated into Italian, American publications reached a public which until then had read very little. In other fields, American analytical methods opened new vistas to Italian social scientists, among whom deductive and *a priori* methods had long prevailed over inductive and scientific methods; and Italian-trained scientists did valuable work, in physics and biology especially.

What abolition of censorship did for the activities of the mind, abolition of the rigid institutional structure imposed on the economy by fascism did for material activities. Whatever the formal institutions existing on paper or advocated by dominant political forces, for two decades Italy has had both economic liberty and a willingness to make use of it. This liberty was not something Italians had wanted: it was the result of the collapse of Fascist corporatism and of the general disruption caused by invasions, wars, and revolutions. Economic recovery began in the post-Fascist era before the government framework had been reconstructed. It was regulated by a market

which happened to be relatively free. It was the result of the in-
genuity, imagination, and hard work of a sizable minority, including
several million entrepreneurs, some big, most small or very small.

American capital played an important role in Italian postwar recovery. The total of funds of the European Recovery Program made
available to Italians in 1948-52, other funds which improved the economic infrastructure required by military forces, and private investments (to the tune of over a third of a billion dollars in 1958-63)
amounted to three to four billion dollars of American capital injected
into the Italian economy. American trade, which amounted to over
a billion dollars of imports and exports in the early 1960's, American
tourism, and American gifts to Italian Catholic organizations and to
numerous lay institutions helped the Italian economy considerably.

Even considering government participation and American investments, economic achievements were primarily the result of action
taken by the managers of industrial, agricultural, and other enterprises. The population of Italy increased by less than a fifth in twenty
years, while the gross national product in 1964 was more than three
times what it had been in the last normal year before 1945; thus, the
real per capita income increased two and a half times during this
period. The share of agriculture in the national income went down,
but agricultural output increased. Output of manufacturing doubled
in real value between 1953 and 1962; output of services more
than doubled. New construction provided better housing. Foreign
trade, particularly important for Italy, reached in 1962 a sum equivalent to the total prewar national income. As a result Italians ate more
and better. Health conditions improved. There were more dwellings
in relation to the number of families, and more space in the dwellings.
To the dismay of those attached to traditional stagnation, Italians
moved more freely. Physical mobility was a factor in social mobility
and in changing class relationships.

For the first time in four hundred years the whole nation was
emerging from backwardness, the south and not just the north, the
peasantry and not just the business communities. But the hopes of
government leaders—from Bonomi and De Gasperi to Moro and
Saragat—that intellectual awakening and material progress would
cause most Italians to recognize the advantages of free democratic
institutions were only in part realized. Social change, brought about

by a wealth of new experiences as well as by economic expansion, were accompanied by imbalance. New problems cropped up, mainly linked to unfulfilled expectations, large-scale temporary migration to other countries, change in ethical standards. Tension between antagonistic economic and political groupings was considerable in the early 1960's, particularly in 1963-64. Awareness of defects and shortcomings was greater than awareness of merits and achievements. Electoral returns showed that numerous Italians were convinced that democracy was something temporary, to be discarded when occasion arose. In the early 1960's neither communism on the left nor neo-fascism and clericalism on the right were as extreme as their predecessors had been in previous decades, but they were still authoritarian.

The Italian nation successfully overcame the growing pains of the 1890's, but it failed to overcome the growing pains of the post–World War I period. Chances were that the late 1960's would witness a repetition of what had happened seventy, not forty, years earlier. But this was not certain. The survival of democracy depended on the success with which Italy could solve her social and moral problems within the frame of free institutions. On this too depended in great measure the position Italy would occupy on the international chessboard, success leading naturally to closer cooperation with the United States and Western Europe, failure leading to growing neutralism and a rapprochement with adversaries of the United States.

Historical works abound for a nation whose documented history spans nearly three millennia, which has at times exercised considerable influence outside its borders, and in which historical writing has been cultivated since the second century B.C.

Most works on Italian history fall within one of three main groups, according to the authors' basic views of man and society. Like some of their foremost pagan predecessors, Catholic historians see in Italian developments the Divinity's guiding hand and the fulfilment of a Divine plan. Other historians, postulating a creativity with which men are endowed even if few use it, interpret Italy's history as a succession of events that might have been different, because of the role played by man's free will and by myriad chance elements. For the largest group of recent influential historians, the succession of events is an iron chain forged by determining factors—economic, ethico-political, racial, geographical—according to the authors' ideologies. Thus, God, liberty, and necessity are the keystones of the three main groups of scholars who have risen above the level of chroniclers. As there are many interpretations of God, liberty, and necessity, each school embraces many subdivisions. The careful student should avoid restricting himself to one author or one school.

Whatever the point of view, most histories reflect a sympathy for Italy and Italians which tends to alter the Italian scene, at times considerably. This is so in the case of Livy who wrote in the first century B.C., as it is in the case of G. Volpe and of B. Croce, the two leading Italian historians of the twentieth century, and of many non-Italian historians, like de Sismondi and Trevelyan. L. Salvatorelli's *Concise History of Italy From Prehistoric Times to Our Own Days* (1939) is probably the least biased summary of main Italian developments. Foreigners have been fascinated by Italian history: for ancient times the names of two Greeks, Polybius and Plutarch, will suffice; in modern times, British historians have dwelt at length and competently with Italy, from E. Gibbon, T. A. Symonds, and G. M. Trevelyan to H. Acton, F. W. Deakin, and D. Mack Smith; good scholarly works were produced by Germans such as R. Davidsohn, F. Gregorovius, T. Mommsen, L. v. Pastor. Spurred by fellowships and grants, American scholars have recently been writing more and more about Italy, often with greater detachment and objectivity than has been achieved by Italians or other Europeans. Only a few of the many valuable works produced by American scholars will be mentioned in the following pages.

Special mention must be made of works dealing with Italian history that are considered classics; these are on a level at which inaccuracies of detail are amply compensated by breadth of view and by the integration of specific events in a large historical scheme. A limited list of classics would include: T. Livy, *History of Rome*, C. Tacitus, *Annals* and *History*, Plutarch, the biographies of notable Romans in the *Parallel Lives*, T. Mommsen, *History of Rome*, published many times in English since 1870. For the passage from Roman to Catholic Italy, there are relevant volumes and chapters in E. Gibbon, *Decline and Fall of the Roman Empire* (1st ed. 1776). For the Middle Ages and the Renaissance, there are: F. Gregorovius, *History of the City of Rome During the Middle Ages* (trans. from the 4th German ed., 1894-1902); the English condensation, supervised by the author, of S. de Sismondi, *History of the Italian Republics in the Middle Ages* (1st ed., 1832); J. A. Symonds, *The Renaissance in Italy* (1875-1908); J. C. Burckhart, *The Civilization of the Renaissance in Italy* (English ed., 1878); F. Guicciardini, *The History of Italy* (1st English ed., 1599). For the more recent periods, valuable classics are B. Croce, *A History of Italy 1871-1915* (1929) and G. Volpe, *Italia Moderna 1815-1915* (1946).

SOURCES. To the eighteenth-century historian L. Muratori are owed the *Annali d'Italia* (1744-1749), continued well into the twentieth century by A. Coppi, I. Ghiron, P. Vigo. Muratori also published two valuable collections: *Rerum Italicarum Scriptores* (1723-1751) and *Antiquitates Italianae Medii Aevi* (1738-1742). The Italian Historical Institute, established in 1883, in which were merged regional institutes, some functioning since 1833, published a collection of primary sources, *Fonti della Storia d'Italia*. The *Atti Parlamentari* and the collection of *Trattati e Convenzioni* are important sources for the internal and external policies of the Italian state since the 1859-60 unification.

THE ITALIANS. It is useful to know what Italians are and what they have been during crucial phases of their history, before exploring Italy's past. A good starting point is L. Barzini, *The Italians*, a 1964 American bestseller, keeping in mind that the author deals mainly with the types of Italians tourists meet and that therefore the picture is a partial one. Modern Italians in historical perspective is the topic of two books which should be read concurrently: G. A. Borgese, *Goliath, The March of Fas-*

cism (1937) and G. Prezzolini, *The Legacy of Italy* (1948). Borgese's book is written from the viewpoint of a progressive internationalist democrat, Prezzolini's from the viewpoint of a disgruntled nationalist. A good study is L. Olschki, *The Genius of Italy* (1949). Interesting but rather superficial is C. Sforza, *Contemporary Italy, Its Intellectual and Moral Origins* (1944). G. Piovene, *Viaggio in Italia* (1957) contains much detailed information but has not been translated into English. Among historians who have dealt with Roman Italians are J. Carcopino, A. J. Church, H. Mattingly, M. I. Rostovtsev, A. H. Treble. A useful comprehensive short volume is E. Hamilton, *The Roman Way* (1932). Post-Roman Italians in the past have been the topic, among others, of J. C. Burckhardt, *op. cit.*, L. Collison-Morley, *Italy after the Renaissance* (n.d.), B. Croce, *Storia dell'Età Barocca* (1929). Perceptive essays are contained in collections of lectures published as *La Vita Italiana nel Trecento* (1897), *La Vita Italiana nel Rinascimento* (1899), *La Vita Italiana nel Risorgimento* (1897-1901). Aspects of regional life are the topics of U. Boncompagni-Ludovisi, *Roma nel Rinascimento* (1928), P. Molmenti, *La Storia di Venezia nella vita privata dalle origini alla caduta della repubblica* (1927), V. and E. Verga, *Storia della Vita Milanese* (1931).

GENERAL HISTORIES. The *Storia d'Italia* planned by P. Fedele was published in nine volumes, 1936-1962. The volumes contain the basic factual information but they are uneven, as is often the case with works written by a team of authors. Less uneven was the older *Storia Politica D'Italia*, planned by L. Villari and published in eleven volumes, 1874-1882. The chapters concerning Italy in the volumes of the *Cambridge Ancient, Medieval,* and *Modern History* give a comprehensive and detailed account of Italian developments. One-volume good comprehensive histories are L. Salvatorelli, *op. cit.*, and C. Balbo, *Sommario della Storia d'Italia*, continued by A. Solmi (1927). Among recent short histories of Italy, based on secondary sources only and aimed at the general public, are those by J. P. Trevelyan (rev. ed., 1951), H. Hearder and D. P. Waley (1963), and G. Trease (1964). Histories of Italian literature by F. De Sanctis (revised by B. Croce, 1912), and by F. Flora (1948), deal with literature in its social and political context. The many-volume *Letteratura Italiana: Storia e Testi* began to be published in 1951 and will include 83 volumes. A. Venturi, *Storia dell'Arte Italiana* (1901-1940), was summarized in English in A. Venturi, *A Short History of Italian Art* (1926).

ANCIENT HISTORY. Until the break-up of the Roman Empire in the West, the history of Italy is the history of ancient Rome. For the period prior to Roman rule, the best work is E. Pais, *Storia dell'Italia antica e della Sicilia per l'età anteriore al dominio romano* (2nd rev. ed., 1933). Pais was the most competent twentieth-century Italian historian of ancient Italy; particularly valuable are his *Ancient Italy: Historical and Geographical Investigations* (1908) and books covering the history of Rome from the origins to the late empire, published between 1927 and 1938. T. Mommsen has long been acknowledged as the foremost modern historian of Rome until the end of the Republic. His *History of Rome*, first published in German in 1854-56, has had many editions in English translations. For Italy during the imperial period, there are chapters in E. Gibbon, *op. cit.*, and in J. B. Bury, *History of the Later Roman Empire* (1889). More recent is R. Thomsen, *The Italic Regions from Augustus to the Lombard Invasion* (1947). Volume II of M. I. Rostovtsev, *A History of the Ancient World* (1928) deals with Rome; by the same author is *The Social and Economic History of the Roman Empire* (rev. ed., 1957). G. Ferrero, *The Greatness and Decline of Rome* appeared in English translation in 1907-9. The one-volume G. Ferrero and C. Barbagallo, *A Short History of Rome* was published in 1918-19. The excellent *Storia dei Romani* (1907-1953) by G. de Sanctis was not completed and has not been translated into English.

MIDDLE AGES AND RENAISSANCE. A good, many-volume history of Italy from the fourth to the sixteenth century is provided by the works of three authors: T. Hodgkin, *Italy and Her Invaders* (1892-1899), S. de Sismondi, *op. cit.*, and J. A. Symonds, *op. cit.* A comprehensive one-volume history of Italy in the Middle Ages is H. B. Cotterill, *Medieval Italy during a Thousand Years 305-1313* (1915). Foremost Italian historians of the Middle Ages are P. Villari, whose *The Barbarian Invasions in Italy* (1902), *Medieval Italy from Charlemagne to Henry VII* (1910), and *The Life and Times of Niccolò Machiavelli* (1892) have been translated into English; and G. Volpe who studied Italian Medieval communities, besides being the author of the comprehensive one-volume *Il Medioevo* (1926). L. Salvatorelli, *L'Italia Medievale* (1938) and *L'Italia Comunale* (1940) are on a more popular level and less imbued with nationalistic fervor than the works of Villari and Volpe. On the Renaissance, besides the works of J. C. Burckhardt and J. A. Symonds already mentioned, there is the lively and informative fifth volume *The Renaissance* (1953), in W. Durant, *The History of Civilization*. Among works by Italian historians not available in English are: F. Chabod, *Il Rinascimento* (1942), C. Cipolla, *Storia delle Signorie Italiane dal 1313 al 1530* (n.d.), F. Ercole, *Da Carlo VIII a Carlo V* (1933), L. Simeoni, *Le Signorie* (1950).

MODERN TIMES. The best comprehensive histories of Italy during the period of foreign dominations are A. Visconti, *L'Italia nell'Epoca della Controriforma* (1958), F. Valsecchi, *L'Italia nel Settecento* (1959), and the older A. Cosci, *L'Italia durante le Preponderanze Straniere dal 1530 al 1789* (1875-78). In his great *History of the Council of Trent* (Eng. tr., 1676), P. Sarpi dealt with the crisis that transformed the Italian nation during the sixteenth century and from which was born modern Italy. Sarpi's work should be read conjointly with D. Cantimori, *Per la Storia degli Eretici Italiani del secolo XVI in Europa* (1937), and other works by the same author on Italian religious reformers; also with P. Tacchi

Venturi, *Storia della Compagnia di Gesu in Italia* (2nd ed., 1931). The slow reawakening of the nation in the eighteenth century is the topic of F. Lemmi, *Le Origini del Risorgimento Italiano* (1906), and of A. M. Ghisalberti, *Gli Albori del Risorgimento Italiano* (1931). A useful Chronicle is the older C. Botta's *Storia d'Italia dal 1786 al 1814* (1824).

In the historical scheme applicable to Italy, the years 1815-1965 form a whole: it is the period of struggle for independence, also for and against internal liberty. Two works by British historians competently cover the century and a half: B. King, *A History of Italian Unity* (1899) and D. Mack Smith, Italy: *A Modern History* (1959). One-volume histories are A. J. Whyte, *The Evolution of Modern Italy* (1943) and R. Albrecht-Carrié, *Italy from Napoleon to Mussolini* (1950). C. Volpe, *Italia Moderna 1815-1915* (1946), and F. Lemmi, *Il Popolo italiano dal 1815 al 1899* (n.d.), have treated the nineteenth century as an organic unit; translated into English in several editions, popular and superficial, is P. Orsi, *A History of Italy 1748-1898* (1900). W. R. Thayer, *The Dawn of Italian Independence* (1893), is another work valuable for the pre-independence period. Highly impressionistic and readable are J. W. Mario, *The Birth of Modern Italy* (1909), and J. A. R. Marriot, *Makers of Modern Italy* (rev. ed., 1931). Regrettably A. Omedeo, *L'Età del Risorgimento Italiano* (1932) has not been translated. G. M. Trevelyan's many works on Risorgimento heroes like Garibaldi and Manin are colorful history and fascinating reading. B. King and W. R. Thayer wrote excellent studies of Mazzini and Cavour respectively. More recent are the works of D. Mack Smith on Garibaldi, of G. Salvemini and E. E. Y. Hales on Mazzini (one admiring, the other critical), all published in 1956. Valuable for students is C. F. Delzell, Ed., *The Unification of Italy 1959-61; Cavour, Mazzini or Garibaldi?* (1965). Carefully detailed is the *Storia del Risorgimento e dell'Unità d'Italia* (1933-): the first volumes are by C. Spellanzoa; since his death the work has been continued by E. di Nolfo. Pre- and post-unification Italy is the topic of A. Solmi, *The Making of Modern Italy* (1925), and of C. Barbagallo, *Cento Anni di Vita Italiana 1848-1949* (1948-49). B. Croce's already mentioned *A History of Italy 1871-1915* (1929), is modern historical writing at its best. State-church relations are dealt with objectively in S. W. Halperin, *Italy and the Vatican at War* (1939), and A. C. Jemolo, *Church and State in Italy, 1850-1950* (1960), and less impartially in E. E. Y. Hales, *Pio Nono: A Study in European Politics and Religion in the Nineteenth Century* (1954) and *Revolution and Papacy 1769-1846* (1960). S. B. Clough, *Economic History of Modern Italy* (1964) is the only comprehensive survey of Italy's economy since unification available in English.

For the twentieth century, besides the relevant chapters in works mentioned above, particularly valuable are A. W. Salomone, *Italian Democracy in the Making, 1900-1914* (1945), G. Perticone, *L'Italia Contemporanea 1918-1948* (1961), and L. Salvatorelli and G. Mira, *Storia del Fascismo, l'Italia dal 1919 al 1945* (1952). C. J. S. Sprigge, *The Development of Modern Italy* (1944) is concerned mainly with Italian Fascism in its historical perspective. H. S. Hughes, *The United States and Italy* (2nd ed. 1964) is of course of particular interest to Americans. Written on Italian Fascism from a Fascist point of view are: L. Villari, *The Awakening of Italy* (1924), H. G. Goad, *The Making of the Corporate State* (1934), G. Volpe, *History of the Fascist Movement* (1934), G. Gentile, *Origini e Dottrina del Fascismo* (3rd rev. ed. 1934), G. Pini, F. Bresadda and G. Giacchero, *Storia del Fascismo* (3rd rev. ed., 1940). Critical of Fascism are: G. A. Borgese, *op. cit.*, L. Sturzo, *Italy and Fascism* (1926), and many works by G. Salvemini, among which the most comprehensive is *Under the Axe of Fascism* (1936). Fascist corporate economy within its political context is discussed in C. T. Schmidt, *The Plough and the Sword* (1938) and *The Corporate State in Action: Italy under Fascism* (1939). State-church relationships during the Fascist period are described interpretively in R. A. Webster, *The Cross and the Fasces: Christian Democracy and Fascism in Italy* (1960). Fascist foreign policy is discussed in G. Salvemini, *Prelude to World War II* (1954). There is as yet no good history of the Italian Resistance of 1943-45 in English; in Italian the best factual and interpretive account is C. L. Ragghianti, *Disegno della Liberazione Italiana* (rev. ed. 1962). Antifascism is studied in C. F. Delzell, *Mussolini's Enemies* (1961), and Fascism during the Resistance period in F. W. Deakin, *The Brutal Friendship* (1962). For the recent republican period are available N. Kogon, *The Government of Italy* (1962) and *The Politics of Italian Foreign Policy* (1963).

REGIONAL HISTORIES. Some of the best historical writing concerns Italy's regional states. Florence has had as historians her own sons, G. Villani, *Nuova Cronica* (partial Eng. tr., 1896), written in the fourteenth century; N. Machiavelli, *History of Florence since the earliest times to the death of Lorenzo the Magnificent* (Eng. tr., 1901); C. Capponi, *Storia della Repubblica di Firenze* (1875). In the nineteenth century appeared uneven histories of Florence by the German R. Davidsohn, the Frenchman F-T. Perrens, the Englishman T. A. Trollope. A one-volume comprehensive history of Florence (and Tuscany) is F. Schevill, *History of Florence* (1936). For Genoa there is V. A. Vitale, *Breviario di Storia di Genova* (1955). A. Visconti and A. Molinari, *Storia di Milano* (1937) is the history of much of northern Italy. The older *Storia di Milano* (1783-1798) by P. Verri is valuable. The Kingdom of Naples has been the topic of many valuable studies: P. Giannone, *Istoria Civile del Regno di Napoli* (1723) was continued by P. Colletta, *Storia del Reame di Napoli* (1834). The best one-volume history of Naples is B. Croce, *Storia del Regno di Napoli* (1931). Rehabilitation was the object of H. Acton, *The Bourbons of Naples* (1956) and *The Last Bourbons of Naples* (1961). Piedmont had among its historians E. Ricotti, *Storia della Monarchia Piemontese* (1861-

1869). For Rome under Papal rule, F. Gregorovius, *op. cit.*, was continued less critically by L. v. Pastor, *History of the Popes from the Close of the Middle Ages* (1898). For Sicily there is G. E. Di-Blasi, *Storia della Sicilia* (1861-1864) and the many works dealing with Sicily as independent Moslem and later Christian state by the greatest Sicilian historian, M. Amari. For the Venetian Republic, the best work is P. Molmenti, *Venice* (1906-1908). Less detailed histories are W. C. Hazlitt, *The Venetian Republic 1421-1797* (1900) and W. R. Thayer, *A Short History of Venice* (1905). Valuable recent works on Venetian history by R. Cessi, M. Dazzi, P. Romanin and others have not been translated.

GLOSSARY

Carbonari (charcoal burners): members of the *carboneria*.

Carboneria: clandestine revolutionary society aiming at creating a unified constitutional state in Italy during the immediate post-Napoleonic era. The 1820s were the years of its greatest activity. Liberals, democrats, and other patriots joined the *carboneria* but most democrats (republicans) seceded when Mazzini established the Young Italy clandestine society.

Christian Democracy: that section of Italian political Catholicism which accepts democratic procedure. The passage from authoritarian clericalism to Christian democracy began in the 1890s and progressed in the measure in which it was encouraged by the papacy.

Clericalism: the position of Italian Catholics favorable to Church control over all aspects of national life.

Communism: *see* Revolutionary socialists. After World War II Italian communists gradually became less extremist. After the death of Togliatti in 1964 (appointed as leader by Bukharin in 1926), various factions competed for control of the party; this was supported by about 25 per cent of the electorate.

Comuni: medieval self-governing local communities (city-states), democratic or semidemocratic and *de facto* independent. There were already *comuni* in the 8th century in southern Italy, but they flourished particularly in northern and central Italy from the 11th to the early 14th century. The republic of San Marino is a relic of Italy's communal age.

Conciliatoristi: in the 1530s and 1540s the faction among Catholic cardinals favorable to a compromise with Protestantism. Eliminated at the

Council of Trent (1545-1564), the faction revived at the Council Vatican II (1862-1965).

Corporatism: Catholic formula for the organization of the economy, evolved at the end of the 19th century, adopted by Italian fascism in the early 1920s. In corporatism the means of production and exchange are owned mainly by private interests but the use of them is determined mainly by the state.

Democrats: (a) At the end of the 18th century, the Italian admirers of French Jacobinism. (b) For nearly two generations, from the 1830s on, both the followers of Mazzini's monistic republicanism and the supporters of free institutions founded on universal suffrage were called democrats (or republicans). (c) Since the end of the 19th century, in Italy the term democrat has a meaning similar to that in English-speaking nations (universal suffrage, equality of civil rights, equality of opportunity, secularism, New Dealism in economic and social affairs, internationalism).

Destra (Right): Constitutional conservatives in post-unification Italy. In power 1861-1876, they later merged as Liberals with the *Sinistra*.

Estrema (Extreme Left): pre-World War I republican and socialist deputies opposed to the parliamentarian monarchical regime established in 1861.

Fasci: from the Latin *fasces* (bundle, symbolic of union). The terms *fasci* and *fasciti* were first used at the end of the 19th century by groups of revolutionary socialists; later by groups favoring Italy's active participation in World War I. The *Fasci di Combattimento* (Fighting Unions) founded in 1919 later became the Italian Fascist party.

Fascism: movement which combined aspirations of revolutionary socialism and of integral nationalism, and saw in the totalitarian state the instrument for achieving the greatness of the national community. Political despotism, economic autarchy, nationalist frenzy, violence, and intellectual dogmatism were the key elements of Italian fascism.

Fiancheggiatori: during the period of the Fascist struggle for power and of Fascist ascendance (1920-1945), the name given to those who, though not sharing Fascist values, concepts and aspirations, supported fascism.

Freemasonry: clandestine organization of liberal-minded people, which originated in England and by the middle of the 18th century had spread to many parts of Italy. Religious tolerance, undogmatic rationalism, constitutionalism were among its basic principles. It opposed political despotism both native and alien, and Catholicism. After the unification of Italy freemasonry degenerated, becoming a political machine.

Ghibellines: supporters of imperial (secular) against papal (clerical) authority in the 13th and 14th centuries. Name derives from Waiblingen, headquarters of a faction in the German civil wars that followed the death of emperor Henry V (1125).

Guelphs: supporters of papal (clerical) against imperial (secular) authority in the 13th and 14th centuries. Name derives from Welf, family leading one faction in the German civil wars that followed the death of emperor Henry V (1125).

Humanism: position of the section of Italian intelligentsia during the Renaissance period, more concerned with human affairs than with theological problems. The dignity of man, respect for the individual, tolerance, moderation, and reasonableness were key elements in humanism. A not altogether correct interpretation of ancient authors (Latin and Greek) provided the justification for the humanists' position. To medieval thought, dogmatic and theocratic, they opposed ancient secular thought.

Index: list of books and other publications forbidden by Catholic authorities. Preceded by partial lists, the first comprehensive Index was issued in 1559.

Irredentismo: in post-unification Italy, movement aiming at the annexation of areas ethnically, geographically, or historically Italian belong to other states. Before World War I Austrian-held Trent and Trieste were the main focus of irredentismo; other areas claimed by all or sections of irredentisti were Fiume (Rijeka), Slavic Dalmatia, French-held Nice and Corsica, Malta, and Swiss valleys south of the Alps. In the 1920s irredentismo merged into fascism and gave stimulus to fascist imperialism.

Kingdom of Italy: (a) Medieval: Lombard (568-774), included most of northern Italy and parts of central and southern peninsular Italy; post-Lombard (under Frankish, Italian, and German Kings), included northern Italy except for territories of the Republic of Venice, and the non-papal areas of central Italy. The Peace of Constance (1183) ended de facto the medieval kingdom of Italy. (b) Napoleonic (1805-1814): included less than one third of Italy (much of northern Italy and a smaller area of central Italy). (c) Contemporary (1861-1946): the result of the annexation to the kingdom of Sardinia of Lombardy (1859), most of central Italy (1860), and southern Italy (1860). Proclaimed March 1861. Later additions: Venetia (1866), Latium (1870), Trentino-Alto-Adige, Julian Venetia, and small areas of Dalmatia (1918).

Kingdom of Sardinia: official name of the state ruled by the House of Savoy after the island of Sardinia was added in 1720 to their possessions in north-western Italy and south-eastern France. Also referred to as Savoy, from the name of the ruling house and the region it originally held, and, as Piedmont, from the name of the major component of the state.

Kingdom of the Two Sicilies: the Italian southern state, from the union of Sicily and Apulia early in the 12th century to Sicily's secession (1282). Approximately the same areas 1816-1860.

Liberalism: (a) After French control in Italy ended (1814) the opponents of native traditionalism and foreign domination were called liberals generically. (b) In 1848 and after, Liberals were the progressive moderates who stood for unification of the country under a parliamentarian constitutional regime headed by the House of Savoy, for equality of civil rights, for limited but gradually expanding suffrage, for free enterprise and for secularism (separation of church and state). (c) After World War II the position of Italian Liberals roughly corresponds to that of American constitutional conservatives.

Massimalisti: the pre-Fascist majority section of the Italian Marxist socialist movement. Their program was a *maximum* (hence the name): integral collectivism and democratic organization of the collectivist society. They rejected the notion of a socialist movement achieving success within the frame of a democratic non-collectivist society. Today, the position of the *massimalisti* corresponds approximately to that of the PSIUP (Socialist Proletarian party) supported in 1964-65 by about 3 per cent of the Italian electorate, a close ally of the Communist party.

Mezzadria: until recently the system of land tenure prevailing in most of central Italy and in parts of northern Italy. Traditionally, in *mezzadria*, the landowner provided the capital and paid all expenses except for labor, the peasant provided labor, and the output was divided in half.

Minimalisti: the pre-1914 wing of the Italian socialist movement satisfied with a minimal program: social and economic reforms within a frame of constitutional (bourgeois) democracy and of free enterprise. The ideological position did not differ essentially from that of post-World War II socialdemocrats. In their practical program, the position of the *minimalisti* (as also that of *riformisti*, socialdemocrats and other revisionists) did not differ essentially from that of Italian Radicals and other anti-collectivist democrats.

Neo-Guelphs: expression used in the 1840s to denote liberal-minded, nationalist Catholics. Forerunners of 20th-century Christian Democrats.

Papal states: from the middle of the 8th century to 1859 included about half of central Italy (Latium, Marches, Umbria) and Romagna in northern Italy. Capital, Rome. During much of the Middle Ages existed more in name than in fact. Suppressed for a few years by

Napoleon. Romagna was lost to Sardinia in 1859, Marches and Umbria in 1860. Latium, with Rome, was annexed to Italy in 1870. Revived as Vatican City in 1929.

Piedmont: (a) A large region in north-western Italy. (b) Because Piedmont was the most important area of the duchy of Savoy (after 1720 the kingdom of Sardinia), from the 15th century on the duchy and its successor, the kingdom of Sardinia, were often called Piedmont.

Podestà: chief executive in Italian medieval city-states during the period of transition from democratic to dictatorial regimes (13th-14th century). Under the Fascist regime the government-appointed heads of municipal administrations were called *podestà*.

Principati: *see Signorie*. In becoming hereditary, *signorie* (dictatorships) were changed into *principati*. The change was usually sanctioned by the concession, by emperors or popes, of titles such as duke, prince, marquis.

Regionalism: loyalty to one of the twenty regions into which Italy is divided. Regionalism is the foundation of federalist tendencies among Italians.

Renaissance: the rebirth of intellectual life in Italy in the 14th, 15th, and early 16th centuries. The Renaissance is best known to us today through its artistic manifestations. Actually it was a whole way of life of the non-traditionalist educated classes in Italy.

Resistance: the anti-fascist and anti-German insurgence in German-occupied Italy in 1943-45.

Revisionism: tendency within the Italian socialist movement which accepted the tenets of intellectual liberalism and the institutions of political liberalism.

Revolutionary socialists: before 1914 a term applied to (a) the minority revolutionary wing of Italian Marxism, (b) the syndicalists, (c) the anarchists and anarco-syndicalists. After World War I (a) became the Italian Communist party (1921), (b) provided (together with the Nationalist party) fascism with much of its early membership, (c) dwindled to negligible numbers. Marxist revolutionary socialists were for integral collectivism and total dictatorship, both to be set up through violence.

Riformisti: *see Minimalisti*. *Riformisti* socialists willing to compromise on economic questions (collectivism) but not on political ones (democracy).

Rigoristi: faction among Catholic cardinals in the 1530s and 1540s opposed to any compromise with Protestantism. It triumphed with the Council of Trent (1545-1564), the Roman Inquisition (1542), the Index (1559), the *Confessio Fidei Iridentina* (1564).

Risorgimento: post-Napoleonic movement aiming at the establishment of an independent Italian state founded on free institutions. Conventionally it covers the years 1815-1870.

Savoy: (a) Region in south-eastern France. (b) Family which ruled the county, later duchy, of Savoy. With Victor Amadeus II the dukes of Savoy became kings of Sardinia in 1720, and with Victor Emmanuel II kings of Italy in 1861.

Serenissima: name by which the republic of Venice was known from the late Middle Ages until 1797.

Signorie: dictatorships which from the 13th century on gradually replaced the democratic or semi-democratic regimes of medieval Italian city-states (*see Comuni*). Some dictatorships were oligarchic, most were monarchic and in the 15th century were transformed into *principati*. The principality of Monaco is a relic of Italy's age of *signorie*.

Sinistra (Left): Constitutional democrats in post-unification Italy. In power 1876-1891, they later merged as Liberals with the *Destra*.

Socialdemocrats: *see Minimalisti* and *Riformisti*.

Traditionalism: position in the 18th and 19th centuries of the upholders of Catholic paramountcy, of political despotism, native and alien, of religious intolerance, of Church-controlled intellectual dogmatism.

Trasformismo: the difficult process of political realignment in post-unification Italy. Examples of *trasformismo* have been: the passage from republican to monarchical parliamentarianism of democrats and of radicals around 1900; the acceptance of democracy by groups of socialists in the 20th century.

Vatican: (a) Vast Medieval and Renaissance palace in Rome which at times was residence of the popes. (b) As papal residence since 1870 Vatican came to mean papacy. (c) As headquarters of the papal administration since 1870 Vatican came to denote the central authority of the Catholic church. (d) The palace gives its name to the independent *Città del Vaticano*, established 1929.

Vicari: imperial and papal officials respectively in the kingdom of Italy and the papal states during the late Middle Ages. Usually their authority was nominal. The title of *vicario* at times gave legitimacy to the dictatorial rule of *signori* in the city-states of northern and central Italy.

Young Italy: a clandestine society, nationalist and democratic, founded by G. Mazzini in 1831. Mazzini was also the founder of Young Europe of which, among others, Young Italy, Young Ireland, and Young Hungary were members.

INDEX